Costa Rica

Costa Rica

Revised Edition

BY MARION MORRISON

Enchantment of the World
Second Series

Children's Press®

A Division of Scholastic Inc.

NEW YORK   TORONTO   LONDON   AUCKLAND   SYDNEY
MEXICO CITY   NEW DELHI   HONG KONG
DANBURY, CONNECTICUT

Frontispiece: Plaza de Juan Rafael Mora, San José

Consultant: Ricky Abisla, International Observer, Civic Council of Grassroots and Indigenous Groups of Honduras

Please note: All statistics are as up-to-date as possible at the time of publication.

Book production by Herman Adler

Library of Congress Cataloging-in-Publication Data

Morrison, Marion.
  Costa Rica, revised edition / by Marion Morrison. — Rev. ed.
    p. cm. — (Enchantment of the world. Second series)
  Includes bibliographical references.
  ISBN-13: 978-0-516-24884-4
  ISBN-10: 0-516-24884-7
  1. Costa Rica—Juvenile literature. I. Title. II. Series.
  F1543.2.M67 2007
  972.86—dc22   2006010384

Costa Rica

Contents

Cover photo:
to come

Planting trees

Ancient pot

Welcome to Costa Rica

FOR MOST OF ITS HISTORY, COSTA RICA KEPT A LOW PROFILE. Few outsiders knew much about the small Central American country. But then, in the middle of the twentieth century, some remarkable and long-sighted decisions put Costa Rica on the map.

In 1948, Costa Rica suffered through a civil war. Following this brief period of violence, Costa Rica abolished its army. In the following decades, much of Central America was torn by war, human rights abuses, and dictatorships. But Costa Rica remained a peaceful, democratic country, going about its own business. It became known as the "Switzerland of Central America." Like Switzerland, a mountainous country in Europe,

Opposite: **Coffee and sugar-cane fields blanket much of central Costa Rica.**

More than three hundred thousand people live in San José today. In 1950, the population was just eighty-seven thousand.

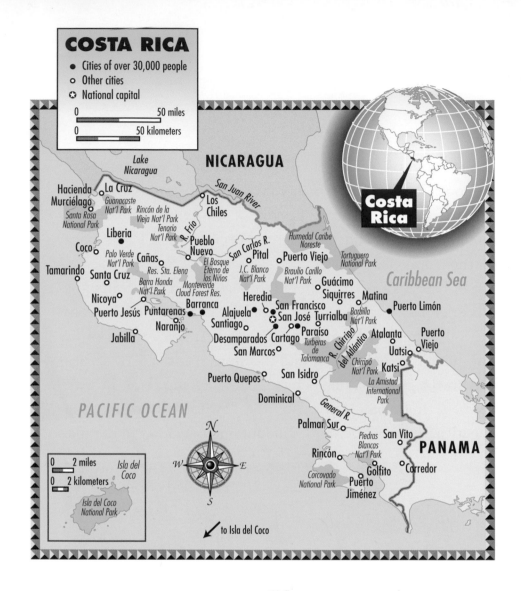

Costa Rica is committed to being peaceful and staying out of the military conflicts that sometimes swirl around it.

Costa Ricans have worked to spread peace in the region. In 1987, the country's president, Oscar Arias Sánchez, worked out a lasting peace treaty that brought an end to a war in the Central American countries. His work earned him the Nobel Peace Prize.

Because of its stable background and democratic traditions, Costa Rica was chosen as the site for the InterAmerican Court of Human Rights in 1979. The University of Peace was also built in Costa Rica. Courses at the university include the study of peace as a way of life, human rights, and issues such as energy and the environment.

In the late twentieth century, Costa Rica also made great efforts to protect its environment. And what a magnificent environment it is! Located at the center of the "bridge" that connects North and South America, Costa Rica is home to a

The monument at the University of Peace honors Costa Ricans' devotion to peace. Each column shows an important moment in Costa Rican history and a leader who helped move the country toward peace.

vast array of plants and animals from both continents. It has twice as many species of trees as there are in the continental United States. The country has dense rain forests, pristine beaches, deep underground caverns, and an amazing variety of life.

At one time, these natural riches faced a great threat from human activity. In the second half of the twentieth century, Costa Rica's population was increasing rapidly. The country was under intense pressure to produce crops and raise cattle, both to feed the growing population and to improve the economy. To make room for agriculture, Costa Rica's magnificent rain forests were being cleared at an alarming rate. The destruction spiraled out of control. By the early 1980s, 322 square miles (835 square kilometers) of forests were being cut down each year.

Then, almost overnight, the tide of destruction was halted. Some Costa Rican leaders realized that the country was in danger of losing its most precious resource—its natural environment. The government produced plans for establishing a large system of national parks and reserves. The country now has 25

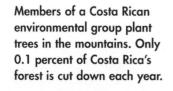

Members of a Costa Rican environmental group plant trees in the mountains. Only 0.1 percent of Costa Rica's forest is cut down each year.

national parks and 136 other reserves, refuges, and protected areas. In all, more than 25 percent of Costa Rica is protected. This is the highest percentage among Western nations.

Today, Costa Rica is one of the world's leading countries in conservation. Since the late 1980s, the government has passed many laws to preserve nature. The country banned open-pit mining. Oil companies are not allowed to drill in the waters off Costa Rica. Landowners are encouraged to farm carefully and to conserve species. The results have been remarkable.

A bridge provides tourists with a treetop view of the Monteverde forest in central Costa Rica. This allows visitors a better chance of spying some of the more than four hundred bird species that live there.

A generation of Costa Ricans has now grown up with the idea that it is important to protect the environment. They are proud that Costa Rica is a worldwide leader in conservation and that it stands as a model for other countries. By protecting nature, Costa Rica has become a magnet for ecotourists. These visitors want to experience the country's natural wonders without harming the environment. And Costa Ricans are happy to offer them a warm and friendly welcome.

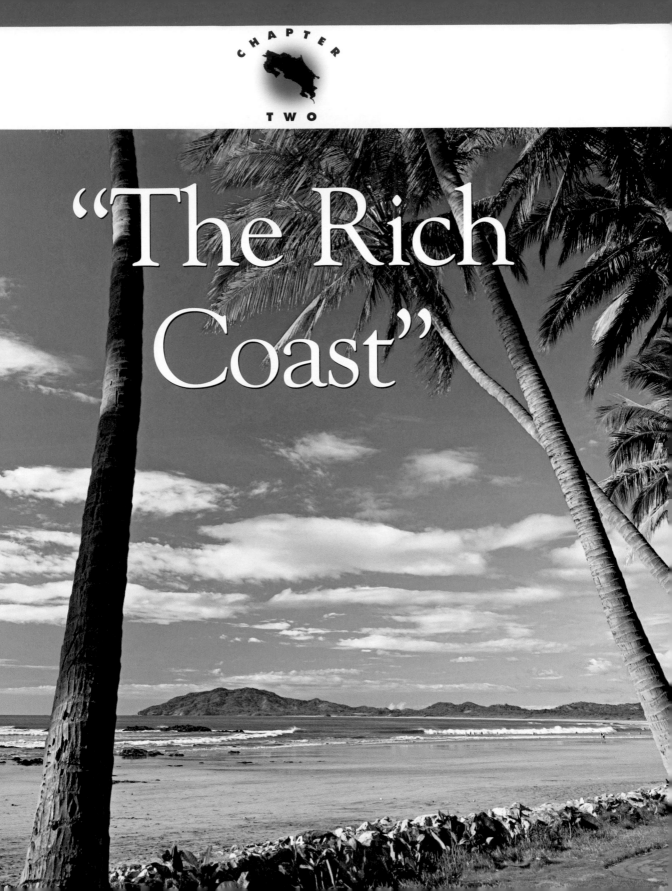

"The Rich Coast"

THE EUROPEAN EXPLORERS WHO FIRST LANDED ON THE Costa Rican coast gave the country its name. Noting how the local people were adorned in gold jewelry, the explorers believed they had found a land of enormous mineral wealth. They called the region *Costa Rica,* "Rich Coast." Once the Europeans realized that the gold did not come from Costa Rica, they left. But they had indeed discovered a rich coast—a land rich in luxurious forests and abundant life.

Costa Rica lies in Central America, the narrow southern part of the North American continent. Nicaragua lies to the north, while Panama is to the south. On the west is the Pacific Ocean, and on the east is the Caribbean Sea, with the Atlantic Ocean beyond. Costa Rica is a small country, slightly smaller than the state of West Virginia. At its narrowest, it is only 74 miles (119 km) wide. The only place where it is shorter to cross Central America is in Panama, which narrows to just 37 miles (60 km).

Opposite: **Nicoya Peninsula on the Pacific coast is a favorite spot for sunbathers and surfers.**

Costa Rica's dense forests are often shrouded in mist.

Costa Rica is part of the so-called ring of fire, a line of volcanoes that roughly circles the Pacific. Through the years, these volcanoes have erupted often. Much of San José, the capital, was covered in ash in 1963 when nearby Irazú erupted. Irazú erupted again in 1994, sending out ash and hot gas. Arenal is one of the most active volcanoes in the world. It had been

Smoke and Fire

Arenal is Costa Rica's most active volcano. It is a perfect cone that rises to 5,437 feet (1,657 m), northwest of San José. The western flank of Arenal rises from Lake Arenal, the largest lake in the country and a popular spot for fishing and sailing. Arenal Volcano first erupted about seven thousand years ago. Since 1968, it has been erupting with lava flows, smoke, and ash almost continuously. A major eruption occurred in 2002 and more spectacular activity began in 2005. Today, many tourists visit Arenal to see the billowing ash and rivers of red-hot lava.

Earthquake Safety Rules

Costa Ricans need to know how to stay safe during the country's frequent earthquakes. Here are some guidelines they are told to follow:

DO

When the shaking starts, get to a doorway, an inside corner wall, or under a desk or table.

Disconnect the electricity as soon as you safely can.

Take pots off the stove.

If you are driving, stop. You could hit a panicky person who runs into the street. Get out of the car and seek shelter in a doorway.

DON'T

Don't rush outside. Outside walls tend to fall outward. Also, windows shatter; trees, poles, and signs topple; roof tiles fall into the street; and power lines come down.

Don't use the telephone. Lines must be kept open so emergency calls can be made.

Don't use elevators or escalators right after a quake.

---

quiet for many years until 1968, when it exploded in an eruption that killed seventy-eight people.

The ring of fire is also prone to earthquakes. Cartago, a historic city close to San José, has been severely damaged by earthquakes three times. The last time, in 1910, was the worst earthquake in Costa Rican history. It left 1,750 people dead. An earthquake on April 22, 1991, pushed the city of Puerto Limón on the Caribbean coast about 3 feet (1 meter) higher above the sea than it had been. The city's highway to San José was destroyed, and the town was isolated for several days.

The Highlands

A chain of mountains curves from the northwest to the southeast across Costa Rica. To the north are the *cordilleras*, or "mountain ranges," of Guanacaste and Tilarán. The volcano Rincón de la Vieja rises to 6,286 feet (1,916 m), dominating the Guanacaste range.

Clouds cover the peaks in the Cordillera de Talamanca in southern Costa Rica. More than 230 inches (600 cm) of rain fall in parts of this range every year.

The Cordillera Central in the center of the country rises to 11,260 feet (3,432 m) at the summit of Irazú, the highest volcano in Costa Rica. A range of hills known as La Carpintera marks the Continental Divide. Rivers to the east of the divide flow to the Caribbean. Rivers to the west flow to the Pacific. One of the major rivers flowing east is the Reventazón. Adventurous tourists love to kayak down the Reventazón as it tumbles through gorges and dense forests on its way to the coast.

In the south stands the Cordillera de Talamanca. Costa Rica's highest mountain, Chirripó Grande, is on the western side of the Cordillera de Talamanca. On clear days, it is possible to see both the Pacific and the Atlantic oceans from its summit at 12,530 feet (3,819 m). Separating the Cordillera de Talamanca from the Pacific Ocean is a lower range of mountains called the Fila Costeña, which means "Coastal Row." Between the Cordillera de Talamanca and the Fila Costeña lies a long fertile valley. The northern section of the valley is

Costa Rica's Geographic Features

Area: 19,730 square miles (51,100 sq km)

Highest Elevation: Chirripó Grande, 12,530 feet (3,819 m)

Lowest Elevation: Sea level, along the coasts

Longest River: Río Grande de Térraba, 122 miles (196 km)

Largest Lake: Lake Arenal

Longest Shared Border: With Panama, 397 miles (639 km)

Largest City: San José, with 336,829 people in 2004

Average Annual Precipitation: 100 inches (254 cm)

called the Valle del General. Pineapples, coffee, and cattle are grown there. The Río Grande de Térraba, Costa Rica's longest river, rises in the Cordillera de Talamanca. It cuts westward through the Fila Costeña and flows into the Pacific.

The Meseta Central

The Cordillera Central overlooks the Meseta Central, which means "Central Plateau." The Meseta Central is a flat area with unusually rich soil. This is the heartland of Costa Rica. In every direction, you can see forested slopes and rolling hills covered in lush, green coffee plants or tall stands of sugarcane. More than half of Costa Rica's four million people live in the valleys of the Meseta Central.

About 10 percent of the land in Costa Rica is used for crops. Most of this land is in the Meseta Central.

A Look at Costa Rica's Cities

Puerto Limón (right), Costa Rica's second-largest city, has a population of 61,200. Located on the Caribbean coast, it is Costa Rica's most important port. The port developed with the construction of a railroad in the 1870s to accommodate the booming banana industry. Today, visitors to Puerto Limón can enjoy views of the sea while strolling beneath palm trees. The town also has a tropical park frequented by two-toed sloths, strange sluggish creatures native to Central and South America.

For more than 250 years, Cartago (below) was the nation's capital. It stands 14 miles (22.5 km) from

the current capital, San José, in the southern Meseta Central. Founded in 1564 at the foot of the Irazú volcano, Cartago never grew large. In 2004, the population was only about 26,000.

In 1841 and 1910, Cartago was severely damaged by earthquakes. Many of its buildings were destroyed. Today, parts of the town have been rebuilt in the Spanish colonial style. Cartago's most famous attraction is the Church of Our Lady of the Angels. It houses a treasured image of Mary, Jesus's mother, which draws visitors from all over the country.

Another popular site near Cartago is the Lankester Gardens. An Englishman named Charles Lankester left the land and his collection of plants to the people of Costa Rica. Hundreds of species of spectacular orchids and bromeliads grace the gardens.

Peaceful beaches abound on the Osa Peninsula on the southern Pacific coast. It is one of the most remote parts of Costa Rica.

The Coasts

For almost the whole length of Costa Rica's Pacific coast, hilly slopes descend straight to the sea. The exception is in the north, where a narrow strip of lowland lies between the sea and the foothills. Much of that land is used to raise cattle.

The Pacific coastline is almost 630 miles (1,015 km) long. This is much longer than it seems on a map because of its many peninsulas and bays. In the far north is the Santa Elena Peninsula. Then comes the largest peninsula, Nicoya, with many miles of sandy beaches that make it a favorite with tourists. In southwestern Costa Rica, the Osa Peninsula is smaller, and Puerto Jiménez is the only town of any size.

The Caribbean coast is only 185 miles (298 km) long. A large triangular area of lowland plains stretches inland from the Caribbean to the border with Nicaragua in the north and to the mountains in the west. These plains seldom rise higher than 300 feet (100 m). The Caribbean coast has fewer good beaches than the Pacific, and swimming is not recommended. The waters have strong currents—and sharks.

Islands

Many islands lie off Costa Rica's Pacific coast. Near the Nicaraguan border is dry, scrubby Isla Bolaños, which is home to many seabirds. The Gulf of Nicoya is the site of many islands with beautiful sandy beaches, the most popular being Isla Tortuga. Isla San Lucas was once used as a prison. Today, tourists can visit the island and wander through the crumbling buildings. The small islands of Guayabo and Negritos are biological reserves.

Isla Tortuga is famed for its white sand beaches and clear blue water.

Two Seasons

In tropical regions like Costa Rica, the weather is usually hot and rainy. In the Meseta Central, temperatures rise to 75 to 80 degrees Fahrenheit (24 to 27 degrees Celsius) throughout the year. The Caribbean lowlands are much hotter. There, the average high temperature is about 100°F (38°C). March through May are the hottest months.

A Distant Paradise

Isla del Coco is Costa Rica's most famous island. It is about 7.5 miles long and 3 miles wide (12 by 5 km) and lies more than 300 miles (480 km) southwest of the mainland. The island is rugged, mountainous, and covered with forests. Tall cliffs rising more than 300 feet (100 m) ring much of the island, and waterfalls abound. At the western end, the land rises abruptly to Yglesias Hill, the island's highest point. Pirates and early explorers are said to have used the hill as a lookout, and there are many stories of buried treasure. Dozens of treasure hunters have tried their luck, but so far they have found nothing.

During the early twentieth century, a few people brought pigs, planted coffee, and tried to settle on the island. But they did not succeed. The land is rocky, hilly, and heavily wooded, so it is not easy to farm. No one lives there now, making it possibly the world's largest uninhabited island.

Today, Isla del Coco has been set aside as a national park. It is rarely visited, however, because it is expensive to get there. A few tourists make the journey since it is a top scuba diving spot. Scientists also go to the island to study the wildlife. Of special interest are some species found only on the island, including three birds: the Coco Island cuckoo, the Coco Island finch, and the ridgeway flycatcher.

Costa Ricans say they have two seasons: wet and dry. The wet season is between May and November, and the dry season lasts for the rest of the year. Even during the wet season, the sun usually shines until midday in San José. Then, in mid-afternoon, there might be a tremendous drenching rain for an hour or two.

Winds also affect the climate, and the Costa Ricans give them special names. The *norte* is a cool wind from North America that sometimes reaches Costa Rica between November and January, lowering temperatures for a few days. The *papagayos* are strong winds that blow in from the Pacific, and the *alisios* are the winds that affect the northern slopes along the Pacific.

The wettest months along the Pacific coast are September and October. During this time, huge storm clouds gather and blow across the country.

Amazing Life

EW PLACES ON EARTH HAVE SUCH A VARIETY OF LIFE AS Costa Rica. It has habitats ranging from tropical waters to soaking rain forests to the barren summits of volcanoes.

Costa Rica occupies only 0.03 percent of the world's land surface, yet it is home to an estimated half a million species. About 360,000 of these species are insects. Another 68 are lizards, and 127 are snakes. The latter includes the bushmaster, the largest venomous snake in the Americas, which can grow to 11 feet (3.5 m) long.

Opposite: **Spider monkeys are active during the day. They can often be seen swinging through the tree-tops in damp forests.**

The bite of the bushmaster is deadly. About 80 percent of the people bitten by a bushmaster die.

The National Bird

The *yigüirro*, or clay-colored robin, is Costa Rica's national bird. Though not as showy as many of Costa Rica's birds, it is much loved because it is considered friendly and unafraid of people. It can often be seen in yards and along forest edges.

Costa Rica has 870 types of birds. These range from brightly colored macaws and toucans to harpy eagles that are so big they can eat a monkey. Costa Rica is home to four species of monkeys, three species of anteaters, and six species of

The Quetzal

One bird found in Costa Rica's cooler, higher forests is the resplendent quetzal. This rare bird has glittering blue and green wings and a bright red stomach. The quetzal is found in forests from southern Mexico to western Panama. In many places outside Costa Rica, this spectacular bird is in danger because its habitat is threatened by loggers and farmers.

cats, including the fearsome jaguar. Huge sloths hang from the trees, while tapirs—strange creatures that look like pigs, are related to horses, and have short trunks like elephants— munch on grass and twigs on the ground.

Female three-toed sloths carry their young for six to nine months. Sloths come down from the trees only about once a week.

Astonishing Diversity

To see some of Costa Rica's wealth of species, just travel up a mountainside. As the elevation increases, the rainfall, temperature, sunlight, and soil change—and so do the plants that live there. Different kinds of plants attract different species of animals. This incredible diversity can be seen in many of Costa Rica's national parks.

The National Tree

The guanacaste is Costa Rica's national tree. Often called the elephant's ear tree or monkey ear tree, it gets its nicknames from the brown, ear-shaped seedpods that dangle high in the tree. The pods are used as cattle food. Guanacaste wood is often used for high-quality furniture and boats.

Chirripó National Park surrounds much of Costa Rica's highest mountain, Chirripó Grande, and rises to elevations of about 8,000 feet (2,400 m). The park is a good example of the huge habitat extremes found in just one area of the country. Warm tropical forests blanket the lower levels of the park. But at the rocky summit, it can be below freezing. The mountain slopes facing the Caribbean are always wet. The Pacific side is drier.

Throughout the park are a range of forests, depending on the specific climate and soil. In some places are oak forests. In others are forests with a mix of trees that keep their leaves year-round and trees that do not. There are valleys green with ferns. High on the mountains, only short, hardy plants survive. Elsewhere, the mountainsides are permanently cloaked in clouds. In the wet, dripping cloud forests, every tree seems to be covered with mosses, ferns, and orchids. Many of the plants get the water they need from the air rather than the soil.

Birds also vary with the elevation. They range from the tiniest hummingbirds—which hover over flowers with an almost invisible beating of wings—to magnificent eagles. Chirripó National Park is home to all six members of the cat family found in Costa Rica. The margay is about the size of a house cat, with dark markings on a light brown coat. The other Costa Rican cats are pumas (also known as cougars or mountain lions), ocelots, jaguarundis, oncillas, and jaguars.

The margay cat spends most of its time in the trees. It often hunts birds, monkeys, and squirrels.

The Deepest Park

The Barra Honda National Park includes very different types of habitats. Located about 200 miles (300 km) northwest of San José, the park extends into more than forty underground caverns in the dry northwest of the country. The deepest cavern that has been explored plunges 790 feet (240 m) below the earth's surface. Bats, blind salamanders, fish, cave insects, and specialized plants all live in the darkness of the caverns.

Barra Honda is surrounded by forests of wild plum and wild cotton. Aboveground, the forest is home to white-nosed coatis—racoonlike mammals—and white-faced capuchin monkeys, skunks, and armadillos. Among the many birds are orange-fronted parakeets.

Barra Honda National Park contains the largest cave system in Costa Rica. Only nineteen of the park's forty-two caves have been explored.

The National Flower

The *guaria morada* is Costa Rica's national flower. It is a member of the orchid family. Flower lovers prize orchids for their beautiful and often delicate blooms. The guaria morada, which has bright purple flowers, is the most commonly grown orchid in Costa Rica.

The Monteverde Cloud Forest Reserve

The Monteverde Cloud Forest Reserve was founded in 1986. It protects a large area of cloud forest, a type of forest in which the trees are almost always shrouded in mist. At Monteverde, streams and waterfalls tumble down the slopes. The forest is thick with mosses, ferns, bromeliads, vines, orchids, and many plants.

Small frogs, spiders, leaf-cutting ants, and many other insects live on the dark, damp forest floor. More than four hundred species of birds, including the quetzal, have been found in Monteverde. The park is also home to some five hundred species of butterflies, one hundred mammal species, and more than two thousand kinds of plants.

Beach and Forest

Osa Peninsula in the southwest of Costa Rica is renowned for its stunning beaches. Corcovado National Park, one of Costa Rica's most spectacular parks, was established there in the 1970s.

Corcovado is extremely isolated. Along with the beaches, it includes the only rain forest left in Central America that has never been logged. Corcovado's amazing variety of wildlife includes scarlet macaws, jacamars, white-lipped peccaries (wild pigs), jaguars, giant anteaters, sloths, and squirrel monkeys. Home to 140 species of mammals and 367 species of birds, the park is practically an encyclopedia of Central American nature. Who knows how many secrets or undiscovered species still hide within its forests?

Thousands of olive ridley sea turtles come ashore at the same time to lay their eggs. Within an hour, most have returned to the sea.

Life in Water

The beaches of the Santa Rosa National Park in northwestern Costa Rica are well-known nesting sites for turtles. At the same time every year, thousands of sea turtles return to the beach on which they were hatched to nest and lay their eggs. The turtles' future has been threatened by people who kill the turtles for their eggs and shells. In the 1970s, Costa Rica began a program to save the turtles. Now, when the turtles gather, access to the beaches is restricted.

On the northern Caribbean coast are a series of canals just inland from the sea. These canals were built to connect many of the natural lagoons along the swampy coastline. Today, barges still use these canals to transport bananas and other goods. The lagoons and canals are home to sea cows, which are also called manatees. These large mammals never leave the water.

Some of the lagoons and beaches have been set aside as Tortuguero National Park. *Tortuguero* means "turtle catcher." These beaches are the most important nesting places in the western Caribbean for the endangered green turtle.

Few people visit La Amistad International Park. Those who do might see giant anteaters or all six cat species that live in Costa Rica.

The Friendship Park

La Amistad International Park is Costa Rica's largest park, but it is also the hardest to reach. Most of the park is high in the Cordillera de Talamanca. It is a joint project between Costa Rica and Panama that expresses *amistad*, or "friendship," and cooperation in the cause of environmental protection.

Much of the park has yet to be explored. But already scientists have discovered almost four hundred bird species there. They believe the park has the largest concentration of quetzals in Costa Rica. Many people see La Amistad as a hopeful sign that the idea of conservation will spread throughout Central America and beyond.

Freedom and Peace

The earliest humans in the Americas came from Asia. They crossed the Bering Strait between what are now Russia and Alaska during the Ice Age more than twelve thousand years ago. The first peoples to reach the region that is now Costa Rica were hunter-gatherers. They roamed the valleys and forests hunting game and collecting fruits, nuts, and other edible plant parts. They also fished along the coasts and rivers. Gradually, these early Costa Ricans developed agriculture. By 2000 B.C., they were growing crops such as corn, squash, avocados, and beans.

The oldest pottery in Costa Rica dates from 1000 B.C. to 500 B.C. By that time, some Costa Rican communities had become well organized. They had chiefs, nobles, and priests. People in Costa Rica did not build pyramids or other large monuments such as those built by the Maya people of Mexico and Guatemala. But they had contact with the Maya and with groups from Panama and Colombia. Costa Rica was on the trading route between these two regions.

When Europeans first arrived in Costa Rica in the sixteenth century, an estimated twenty-seven

Opposite: **Costa Ricans celebrate their independence day with a parade of lanterns.**

This pot found in the Nicoya region dates back a thousand years.

The Mystery of the Stone Balls

The Diquis region in southwestern Costa Rica is dotted with large stone balls that are probably about a thousand years old. The balls are perfectly round, and some stand more than 6 feet (2 m) high.

About three hundred of these balls have been found. How did the ancient people carve such perfect balls? What was their purpose? No one today knows the answers.

thousand people lived in the area. Guanacaste in the northwest was the most populated region. The largest group, the Chorotega, lived there. The Catapa, Voto, and Suerre peoples lived in the north, the Cabécar and Bribri lived in the southern Talamanca range, and the Térraba and Boruca lived in the Diquis Valley, in the southwest.

Discovery and Conquest

Christopher Columbus led the first European expedition to reach Costa Rica. In 1502, on his fourth and last trip to the Americas, Columbus was forced by storms to run for shelter. He landed on the Caribbean coast near a village called Cariai, not far from present-day Puerto Limón.

Europeans did not return to Costa Rica until almost twenty years later, when Spaniard Gil González Davila explored most of the length of the Pacific coast on foot. Shortly afterward, Francisco Fernández de Córdova founded the first Spanish settlement in Costa Rica, near present-day Puntarenas. The settlement lasted less than three years, however.

It was almost forty years before the Spaniards began exploring the interior. King Philip II of Spain wanted to found Spanish settlements and begin converting the local people to Christianity. A young lawyer named Juan de Cavallón was charged with settling the interior of the country. In January 1561, he set out from Nicaragua with ninety soldiers and some domestic animals. Three months later, he founded Castillo de Garcimuñoz. He was followed by Juan Vásquez de Coronado, who founded Cartago in 1564.

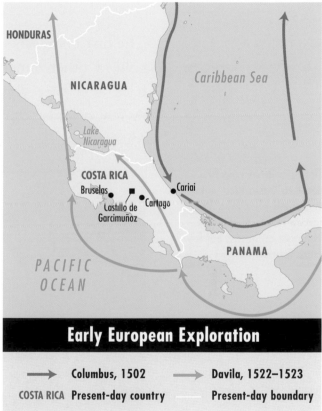

Early European Exploration

→ Columbus, 1502   → Davila, 1522–1523
COSTA RICA Present-day country   Present-day boundary

Many consider Coronado to be the true conqueror of Costa Rica. He was a wise man who used his power well. He made friends with the native people and had some control over them. He was drowned at sea in 1573 while returning to Spain to seek more funds for the small colony.

Colonial Costa Rica

The first European settlers in Costa Rica were hoping to find gold or other minerals. Many settlers lost interest in Costa Rica after they discovered that it held few mineral riches. A few colonists stayed, however, working the land on the Meseta Central.

The Spaniards who first came to Costa Rica were searching for riches. They forced slaves to dig for valuable minerals, but few were found.

The indigenous, or native, people tried to stop these intruders. They resisted the Spanish fiercely, but they had little defense against the Europeans' horses and weapons. Some fled into the dense forests to avoid becoming slaves. Many others died of diseases such as smallpox and influenza, which they caught from the Spaniards. Europeans had long been exposed to these diseases, so their bodies were able to fight them off. The indigenous people had never been exposed to these diseases before, so they had no natural defenses. To them, the diseases were deadly.

Life was hard for the Spanish settlers, and their colony developed slowly. They grew corn, wheat, sugarcane, cacao, tobacco, beans, and cassava. They also raised cattle, horses, and pigs. But their lands and houses were often raided by bands of Miskito Indians from Nicaragua, who destroyed their crops and property.

During the Festival of the Little Devils, indigenous Costa Ricans reenact their struggle against the Spanish colonizers.

From the 1600s to the 1800s, pirates targeted settlers and ships along Costa Rica's Caribbean coast. Some Miskito people joined the pirates in raiding Spanish settlements.

People who settled on the coast did not fare much better. They were constantly raided by French, Dutch, and English pirates. The settlers also had to pay heavy taxes to the Spanish Crown. These were generally paid in cacao beans. In 1709, cacao beans became the official money in the region, and they remained so until the nineteenth century.

In 1723, the volcano Irazú erupted, covering Costa Rica's capital city of Cartago in ash. At that time, the town had only seventy houses, two churches, and two chapels. Costa Rica's total population was fewer than twenty thousand. Both the people and the region were poor.

Costa Rica's lack of mineral wealth saved it from the greed and violence that devastated some of the neighboring colonies. Colonial Costa Rica had no place for social classes, power-hungry officials, or even hatred of the Spanish administration. But these were common elsewhere in Central America and ultimately led to the demand for independence from Spain. The small, backward colony of Costa Rica was swept along in the tide of events.

The United Provinces of Central America

Mexico became independent from Spain in August 1821, and the Central American countries followed one month later. In

1823, Costa Rica joined together with other Central American republics in a federation called the United Provinces of Central America. It was modeled after the United States, where states united to form one nation.

The United Provinces did not last long. Disputes frequently arose between provinces. Costa Rica and Nicaragua argued over the region of Guanacaste. Originally part of Nicaragua, it asked to become part of Costa Rica in 1824. The federation agreed, but the boundary between the two countries was not resolved until 1896. The federation also suffered from constant strain between people who wanted to improve life for all Central Americans and wealthy landowners who wanted to keep power for themselves. Few seemed committed to the federation, and it collapsed by 1840.

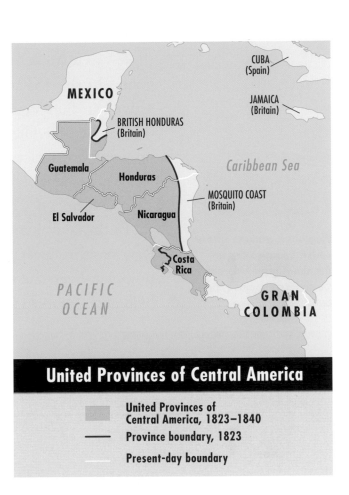

United Provinces of Central America

- United Provinces of Central America, 1823–1840
- Province boundary, 1823
- Present-day boundary

A New Republic

Long before the federation collapsed, Costa Rica had its first constitution, which laid down the laws for governing the country. Juan Mora Fernández was elected the first president and remained in office until 1833. He was largely responsible for introducing coffee into Costa Rica.

It was a stroke of luck that really got the coffee industry going. In the 1840s, English merchant William Le Lacheur arrived in Puntarenas looking for some cargo to take home on his ship. He filled the ship with coffee beans. The coffee proved a great success in Europe, and Le Lacheur became a wealthy man. Soon, British companies began to invest in the Costa Rican coffee industry.

By the mid-nineteenth century, the coffee industry in Costa Rica was thriving. Only a few wealthy Costa Ricans benefited, however. Everyone else remained poor. The wealthy families held great political power and controlled the presidency.

Plantation workers spread coffee beans to dry in the sun. Coffee was already Costa Rica's major export by 1850.

The Walker Affair

The only time Costa Rica has been involved in an international war was between 1856 and 1858. At the time, Juan Rafael Mora, a coffee planter, was president. History remembers him because of the arrival of William Walker (shown right) of Tennessee.

In 1855, Walker had become involved in a civil war in Nicaragua. Walker and his private army quickly took control of the Nicaraguan army, and he declared himself president of that country. Walker was backed by some North American slave traders who offered him men, arms, and money on condition that he introduce slavery into Nicaragua. In March 1856, Walker invaded Costa Rica, planning to take over that country as well.

The Costa Ricans had other ideas. With an army of some nine thousand men, President Mora successfully ousted Walker. He then pursued Walker's men into Nicaragua, defeating Walker at the Battle of Rivas. A great many Costa Rican soldiers died at Rivas, and Juan Santamaría, a drummer boy, became a national

hero when he set fire to an enemy stronghold before he was fatally shot.

Mora was welcomed back to Costa Rica as a national hero. Walker continued to make trouble in other parts of Central America until 1860, when he was executed by a Honduran firing squad.

The Guardia Dictatorship

In 1870, General Tomás Guardia seized power in Costa Rica and established a military dictatorship. He was opposed to the powerful people in the coffee industry who controlled Costa Rica. He replaced them in important positions with his own friends and relatives. He dissolved Congress and in 1871 created a new constitution for governing the country. This constitution lasted until 1949.

This hacienda in Santa Rosa, Costa Rica, was the site of one of President Mora's defeats of Walker's men, who were forced to retreat to Rivas.

Guardia was a harsh dictator, but he also had some liberal ideas. He passed high taxes but used the money to improve the country's education and health systems. He also ended the death penalty long before many other countries did. He is perhaps best remembered, though, as the president who had a railroad built from San José to Puerto Limón, so that coffee could be transported from the highlands to the Caribbean coast.

The Jungle Train

An American named Minor Cooper Keith was responsible for building a railroad through the jungles of Costa Rica so that coffee could be brought to the ports and shipped overseas. Progress on the railroad was slow at first because many workers fell ill with diseases such as malaria and yellow fever. When Keith couldn't find enough Costa Ricans to do the work, he brought in Chinese and Italian laborers. Eventually, he also brought in thousands of black West Indians from the British Caribbean islands to complete the task. It is said that four thousand workers died during the construction of the railroad. But the railroad made Keith a very wealthy man. He invested much of that money in the banana business, which made him even wealthier.

The Costa Rican coffee barons had little interest in the banana business. As a result, the Caribbean banana industry was controlled largely by foreigners. Toward the end of the century, Keith and other American businessmen formed the United Fruit Company, which came to dominate the banana business.

It took nineteen years to build a railroad through the Costa Rican jungle. For taking on the job, the government gave Minor Cooper Keith land along the tracks, which he planted with bananas.

Democracy and Dictators

In the late nineteenth century, most Costa Ricans still had little interest in politics, but democratic ideas were spreading. In 1890, José Joaquín Rodríguez Zeledón won the presidency in what is considered the first entirely free and honest election in Central America.

Two men dominated Costa Rican politics in the early twentieth century—Cleto González Víquez, president from 1906 to 1910 and 1928 to 1932, and Ricardo Jiménez Oreamuno, president from 1910 to 1914, 1924 to 1928, and 1932 to 1936. Although they were political opponents, the two men shared many of the same ideals. They built schools and improved living and working conditions for some Costa Ricans. They also built more roads and bought back land that had been given to the United Fruit Company, which they then distributed to the poor.

Rafael Yglesias Castro became president in 1894. He served two terms.

The next president, Alfred González Flores, tried to change the tax system but was opposed by landowners and businesspeople. He was ousted in 1917 by the Tinoco brothers, Federico and Joaquín. When the Tinocos limited the freedom of the press and jailed their political opponents, many Costa Ricans took to the streets.

Costa Rica's plantation workers toiled long hours and lived in dirty quarters.

Schoolteachers, including many women, and high school students led the way. They set fire to the pro-Tinoco newspaper printing plant. Government troops struck back but made the mistake of firing into the U.S. consulate, where some of the protestors were hiding. The United States threatened to intervene. Before this could happen, the Tinocos fled the country. This kind of dictatorship has never been repeated in Costa Rica.

The Civil War

In the middle of the twentieth century, most Costa Ricans were still extremely poor. Unemployment was high, housing was scarce, workers were badly paid, and many people were ill and poorly fed. Costa Ricans demanded solutions to these problems.

Costa Rican soldiers march through the streets in 1948. More than two thousand people died in the five-week-long civil war.

Rafael Ángel Calderón Guardia won the presidential election of 1940. He introduced far-reaching social reforms and new labor laws. These laws gave workers many rights and ensured that the state would provide for most of their needs, especially if they were ill or out of work. His reforms went way beyond anything known in the region at that time. But soon, Costa Rica's business leaders actively opposed him. He also lost favor with the middle class, who accused him of corruption and fraud.

Calderón had two leading opponents. One was Otilio Ulate Blanco, a newspaper publisher. The other was José Figueres Ferrer, a wealthy landowner and founder of the National Liberation Party. In 1942, Figueres was forced to leave the country for two years after making a radio broadcast fiercely critical of Calderón. When he returned, he decided that military rebellion was the only answer.

Costa Rica had grown chaotic by 1948, as assassinations and street protests spread. Ulate ran against Calderón in the 1948 elections. Figueres was convinced that the elections would be rigged. He asked the president of Guatemala to supply arms. When the ballots were counted, Ulate had ten thousand more votes than Calderón. But, as Figueres had predicted, the National Assembly did not recognize his victory.

The civil war that followed was Costa Rica's darkest hour. Figueres, leading the antigovernment forces, gained control of Cartago and Puerto Limón and eventually surrounded San José. The government forces were poorly trained. Many people died, and the government finally gave in. Calderón fled the country.

A junta (a group of people controlling a government) was formed. It was led by Figueres. The junta governed for eighteen months. Under the junta, a new constitution was written in 1949. This new constitution reformed elections, gave women and blacks the right to vote, and abolished the army. When Ulate took over as president in November 1949, the country was on its way to being a real democracy.

The Father of Costa Rica

José Figueres Ferrer is known as the father of Costa Rica. Figueres was born in 1906, soon after his parents arrived in Costa Rica from Spain. He studied engineering in the United States in the 1920s. Back in Costa Rica, he bought a farm, which he called *La Lucha sin Fin,* meaning "The Struggle without End." It was a strange name for a farm, but most of Figueres's work involved experimenting with new farming techniques and products. He also set up a system that gave his workers a chance to profit from the farm.

After the civil war, Figueres was a national hero. In 1953, he was elected president with 65 percent of the vote. His party, the National Liberation Party, also won a majority of the seats in the National Assembly. President from 1953 to 1958 and again from 1970 to 1974, Figueres ensured that Costa Rica's democratic traditions were firmly established. Figueres died in 1990 at the age of eighty-three.

More Upheaval

Figueres became president in 1953. In 1955, rebels supporting former president Rafael Angel Calderón crossed from Nicaragua into northern Costa Rica. The rebels attacked San José. Figueres, backed by an army of six thousand volunteers, including many high school students, fought them off.

Figueres again served as president in the early 1970s. But when he left office in 1974, the country was deep in debt to foreign banks and organizations. In the coming years, Costa Rica's economic problems increased. Many people were unemployed. Those who had jobs found that prices were rising so fast that the money they earned did not pay for the goods they needed. Eventually, many workers went on strike. The country's economic troubles continued into the 1980s. The government tried to save the country from bankruptcy by increasing taxes and cutting government spending. But this led to more unemployment, strikes, and protests.

Regional Troubles

These were also troubled times for some of Costa Rica's neighbors. In 1979, Nicaraguan dictator Anastasio Somoza was ousted, and a group called the Sandinistas took over the Nicaraguan government. Thousands of refugees fled into Costa Rica. It was the beginning of many years of fighting between the Sandinistas and the *contras* (meaning "those against") who opposed them.

Costa Ricans did not take sides in this war, though it was often difficult to stay neutral. In 1986, President Oscar Arias

Sánchez restored diplomatic relations with Nicaragua and arrested and expelled contras living in Costa Rica.

The following year, he worked out a peace plan to try to settle the military conflicts in Central America. In August 1987, the presidents of El Salvador, Nicaragua, Guatemala, Honduras, and Costa Rica signed the peace agreement. Arias was awarded the 1987 Nobel Peace Prize for his efforts.

Oscar Arias Sánchez became president in 1986. He encouraged tourism and worked to modernize Costa Rica's economy.

Into the Twenty-first Century

In recent years, Costa Rica's economy has improved. Unemployment and poverty have declined, and tourism and other industries are booming. Debt remains a problem, however. Paying only the interest on these loans takes one-third of the country's annual budget. But with a rising standard of living and a peaceful, stable government, Costa Rica remains a beacon of hope in an impoverished region.

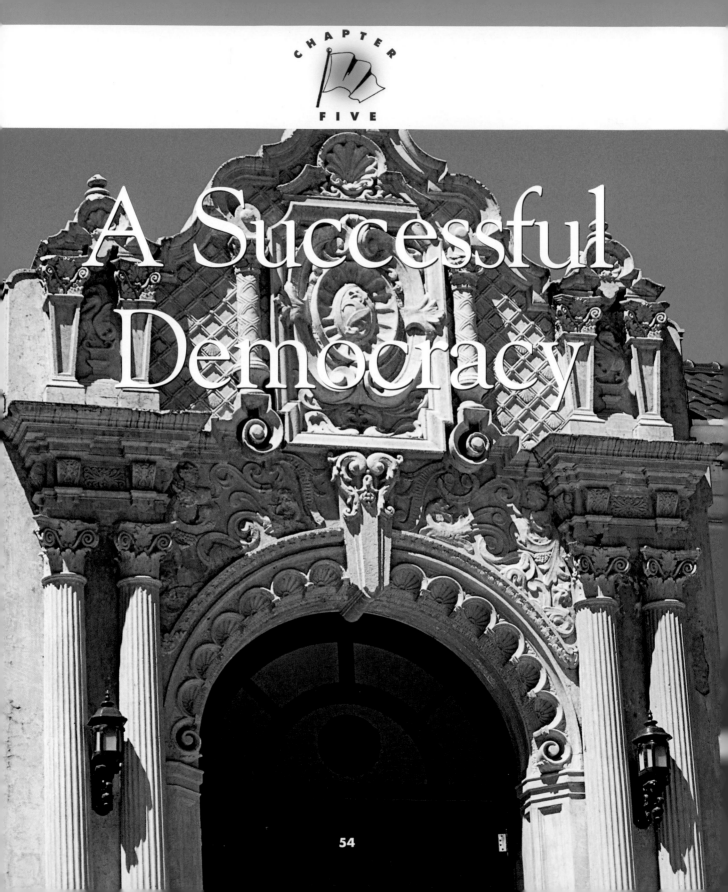

CHAPTER

FIVE

A Successful
Democracy

A woman casts her vote in the 2006 presidential election.

COSTA RICA IS PROUD OF ITS DEMOCRATIC TRADITIONS. It was the first nation in Central America to have free and fair elections, and it remains the most successful democracy in the region. According to Costa Rican law, all citizens age eighteen and over are required to vote. This law is not enforced, however. In the 2006 presidential election, only 64 percent of adults voted. This was the lowest turnout in the history of Costa Rica.

National Government

Costa Rica is governed according to the rules of the 1949 constitution. The government is divided into three branches. The executive branch consists of the president and the cabinet.

Opposite: **The Casa Amarilla ("Yellow House") in San José houses the Department of Foreign Affairs.**

Oscar Arias Sánchez (center) was elected president for the second time in 2006. He chose Laura Chinchilla Miranda and Kevin Casas Zamora as his vice presidents.

The legislative branch is an assembly of representatives elected by the people. The judicial branch is made up of judges and courts.

The president is elected for four years. The president may not be a member of the clergy. To become president, a candidate must receive at least 40 percent of the vote. If no candidate receives 40 percent of the vote, a runoff election is held between the two people with the most votes. This happened for the first time in the 2002 election.

The president is assisted by a first and second vice president and a cabinet of fifteen ministers. If the president resigns or cannot continue in office, the first vice president becomes president. Next in line is the second vice president and then the president of the Legislative Assembly. The president appoints the cabinet of ministers. Each minister is in charge of a different government department, such as Foreign Affairs, Public Security, and Finance. Oscar Arias Sánchez was elected president of Costa Rica in 2006. He also served a term as president in the 1980s.

The Legislative Assembly has fifty-seven members, who are elected by the people to four-year terms. Members of the Legislative Assembly must be Costa Rican and be at least

Costa Rica's Nobel Prize Winner

Oscar Arias Sánchez (second from left) was born into a wealthy Costa Rican family in 1941. He studied law and economics at the University of Costa Rica and earned a doctorate in political science from the University of Essex in England. From 1972 to 1977, he was minister of planning in the national government.

In 1986, at age forty-six, he was elected president for the first time.

As president, Arias moved the economy away from traditional agricultural crops. He also worked to improve education and tried to fight poverty by establishing programs that built houses for low-income families.

While he was president, he negotiated a peace agreement for Central America. He was awarded the 1987 Nobel Peace Prize for his efforts.

Arias ran for president again in 2006 and won. This made him the first Nobel Prize winner to be elected president of any country.

NATIONAL GOVERNMENT OF COSTA RICA

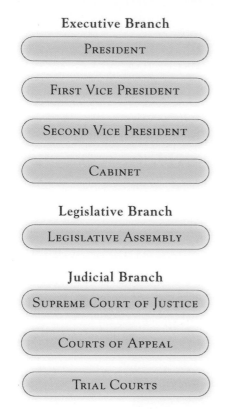

Executive Branch

PRESIDENT

FIRST VICE PRESIDENT

SECOND VICE PRESIDENT

CABINET

Legislative Branch

LEGISLATIVE ASSEMBLY

Judicial Branch

SUPREME COURT OF JUSTICE

COURTS OF APPEAL

TRIAL COURTS

twenty-one years old. They may run for reelection after sitting out one term. The Legislative Assembly has the power to pass laws, impose taxes, and authorize a declaration of war.

The Supreme Court of Justice is made up of twenty-two judges who are elected by the Legislative Assembly. Judges serve for eight years and are normally reelected for another eight years. Judges in the lower courts are appointed by the Supreme Court.

Provincial Government

Costa Rica is divided into seven provinces: San José, Alajuela, Cartago, Heredia, Guanacaste, Puntarenas, and Limón. Each province is divided into cantons. Each canton is governed by a municipal council elected by the people. The council is responsible for all local services except the police. Municipal mayors are also elected by the people.

Keeping Order

The Civil Guard is responsible for enforcing law and order in Costa Rica. The nation's crime rate is relatively low, but illegal drugs are a problem. In 2002, the Civil Guard was made up of

The National Flag

The Costa Rican national flag has five stripes: two blue, two white, and a wide red stripe in the middle. Blue is the color of the sky, white signifies peace, and red represents the cheeks of laborers. Costa Rica's national emblem appears on the red stripe. It depicts three volcanic peaks, the Caribbean Sea, the Pacific Ocean, and two ships. Above the scene are seven stars, which represent the seven provinces.

about 4,400 officers. Costa Rica has the Border Security Police as well, about 2,000 strong. The country has a rural guard and town and village police in the provinces. The president is the chief of all law-enforcement agencies.

Members of the national police stand guard in San José.

Costa Rica's National Anthem

The words to Costa Rica's national anthem, *"Noble Patria, Tu Hermosa Bandera"* ("Noble Homeland, Your Beautiful Flag"), were written by José María Zeledón. The music is by Manuel Maria Gutiérrez.

Spanish Lyrics

Noble patria, tu hermosa bandera
expresión de tu vida nos da;
bajo el límpido azul de tu cielo
blanca y pura descansa la paz.
En la lucha tenaz de fecunda labor
que enrojece del hombre la faz,
conquistaron tus hijos— labriegos
sencillos—eterno prestigio, estima y honor.
(repeat)
¡Salve, oh tierra gentil!
¡Salve, oh madre de amor!
Cuando alguno pretenda tu gloria manchar;
verás a tu pueblo valiente y viril
la tosca herramienta en arma trocar
¡Salve, oh patria! tu pródigo suelo
dulce abrigo y sustento nos da;
bajo el limpido azul de tu cielo
¡vivan siempre el trabajo y la paz!

English Lyrics

Noble homeland, your beautiful flag
expresses for us your life;
under the limpid blue of your skies
peace reigns white and pure.
In the tenacious battle of fruitful toil,
that brings a glow to men's faces,
your sons—simple farmhands—
gained eternal renown, esteem and honor.
(repeat)
Hail, gentle country!
Hail, loving mother!
If anyone should attempt to besmirch your glory;
you will see your people valiant and virile
exchange their rustic tools for weapons.
Hail, oh homeland! Your prodigal soil
gives us sweet sustenance and shelter;
under the limpid blue of your sky
may peaceful labor ever continue!

Relations with the United States

Like most of its neighbors, Costa Rica receives a great deal of financial and technical aid from the United States. Costa Rica relies on the goodwill of the U.S. government in negotiating terms with banks for the loans that support the country's economy. At times, the relationship between the two countries has been strained. In the 1980s, the United States

supported the contras against the Sandinistas in Nicaragua. Because Costa Rica remained neutral in the conflict, the United States cut back on the aid it gave Costa Rica. By 1990, when the Sandinistas failed to win the Nicaraguan elections, good relations between the United States and Costa Rica were restored.

Costa Rican president José María Figueres met with U.S president Bill Clinton in 1997. Figueres is the son of José Figueres Ferrer, "the father of Costa Rica."

San José: Did You Know This?

San José is the capital city of Costa Rica. In 1737, it was just a tiny settlement called Villa Nueva de la Boca del Monte del Valle de Abra ("New Town at the Mouth of the Mountain of the Valley of Abra"). At first, there was little to the town but one small church dedicated to Saint Joseph, who is San José in Spanish. In time, the town became known as San José, and in 1823, it replaced Cartago as the country's capital.

San José sits in the center of the country at 3,773 feet (1,150 m) above sea level. On a clear day, it is possible to see the Poás and Irazú volcanoes from the city. San José is home to the University of Costa Rica, the national theater, and a park named after U.S. president John F. Kennedy, who visited in 1963 on the day that Irazú erupted.

For much of the year, San José has a pleasant climate with springlike temperatures. Because of the city's high altitude, the biggest change in temperature is between day and night, and some evenings can be quite chilly.

In recent years, San José has grown rapidly. In 2004, it had a population of 336,829, and more than a million people now live in the metropolitan area. As more and more people have moved to the city, the number of cars has increased. Today, the city suffers from traffic jams and serious pollution, and the city's air is not nearly as clean as it once was.

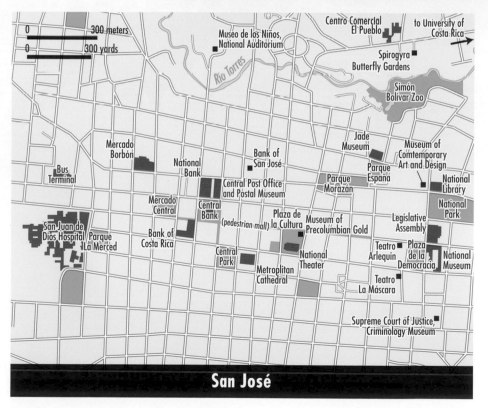

San José

An Expanding Economy

GRICULTURE WAS ONCE THE BASIS OF COSTA RICA'S economy, but now industry and tourism play a larger role. Compared with their Central American neighbors, Costa Ricans have a high standard of living. Only 6.6 percent of the people are without jobs. Restaurants, hotels, supermarkets, and manufacturing industries provide jobs for much of the population. Many people set up fruit and vegetable stands on city streets. On the Meseta Central, most villages and rural areas are involved in the coffee, sugarcane, and dairy industries.

Opposite: **Ships are unloaded at the port of Caldera.**

Costa Rica produces an abundance of fruit, including melons, papayas, and mangoes.

More than 40 percent of Costa Rica's land is devoted to agriculture. In 2005, agriculture accounted for an estimated 8.6 percent of the gross domestic product (GDP), the total value of the goods and services produced in the country. The most important crops are bananas and coffee.

Bananas became a major crop in the late nineteenth century and quickly became the country's leading export. Over the years, disease has sometimes devastated Costa Rica's banana industry. In 1987, disease affected up to 80 percent of

In Costa Rica, most bananas are grown in the Caribbean lowlands. They are the nation's most valuable agricultural export.

What Costa Rica Grows, Makes, and Mines

Agriculture

Sugarcane	3,023,900 metric tons
Bananas	1,863,000 metric tons
Coffee	731,000 metric tons

Manufacturing (value in U.S. dollars)

Food processing	$2,094,000,000
Electronic equipment	$485,000,000
Fertilizer	$260,000,000

Mining

Gold	100 kilograms
Salt	34,733 metric tons

the crop. Since then, the industry has suffered from greater competition on the world market, lower prices, and heavy rains and floods, especially on the Atlantic coast. Still, Costa Rica remains one of the world's largest exporters of bananas. Between 1999 and 2003, the nation supplied an average of about 14 percent of the world's bananas.

Costa Rica was the first country in Central America to produce coffee. The Meseta Central proved to be ideal for coffee growing. It has the right altitude, a good climate, and rich soil. Farmers with even a modest amount of land found they could make a living from the plant. A constant trail of oxcarts was soon transporting the coffee beans from the highlands to the coast. Beginning in the 1840s, Costa Rica regularly exported coffee to Europe, where the drink had become fashionable.

A worker unloads a bucket of coffee beans. About half a million Costa Ricans work picking or processing coffee beans.

Today, most of the coffee in the San José basin and in the Turrialba Valley is grown on a few large coffee plantations. But many small farms produce some of the world's highest yields per acre.

In recent years, Costa Ricans have been growing a greater variety of crops to sell. These include ornamental plants, cut flowers, and tropical fruits. In 2003, pineapples almost

Costa Rican Cowboys

Guanacaste province is the center of the cattle industry in Costa Rica. The cowboys, known as *sabaneros,* were once seen as romantic figures—tough and lonely, herding cattle day and night on the vast plains. Today, they are just as tough and hardworking, but much of the romance has gone.

equaled coffee in export earnings. Cacao, the basis of cocoa and chocolate, is also exported, while cotton is grown to make cloth. The main food crops grown for the home market are rice, corn, and beans.

Chocolate is made from the beans of the cacao tree. Twenty to sixty beans are found in each pod on the tree.

About 1.7 million cattle are raised in Costa Rica.

Costa Rica's cattle industry provides beef for export and dairy products for people in Costa Rica. The most important cattle region is Guanacaste province.

Despite its lengthy coastlines, Costa Rica has only a small fishing industry. The main catches are sardines, tuna, and shrimp. Most of the sardine catch is canned and eaten in Costa Rica. The shrimp is also eaten locally. Tuna is exported, mainly to the United States.

Industry

In 2005, industry accounted for about 28 percent of the GDP. One of Costa Rica's oldest industries is food processing. Fruit, meat, and vegetables are canned, and drinks such as coffee and beer are produced. Today, making chemical products is also big business, as is the manufacture of wood products and textiles. The need for hotels and other facilities to support the tourist industry has given a great boost to the construction industry in recent years.

Since the late 1990s, Costa Rican industry has undergone a significant change of direction. Tax benefits have attracted foreign companies, most based in North America. These companies have invested in factories that make computer parts,

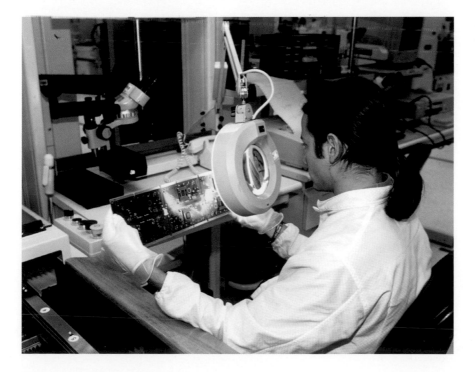

A technician makes computer parts at an Intel Corporation factory in San José. The plant employs almost two thousand workers.

software, and other electronic equipment. This part of the Costa Rican economy is growing rapidly. Exports of electronic equipment and computer goods grew by 52 percent in 2003.

Mining and Energy

Costa Rica has few mineral resources. Limestone is among the leading products. Small quantities of gold, silver, manganese, mercury, and salt are also mined.

Several of Costa Rica's rushing rivers have been dammed to provide hydroelectric power. These power plants provide about 80 percent of the country's energy needs.

Money Facts

Costa Rica's currency is called the colón. It is divided into one hundred céntimos. The government prints banknotes with values of 100, 500, 1,000, 2,000, 5,000, and 10,000 colones. Coins come in values of 1, 2, 5, 10, 25, 50, 100, and 500 colones. In 2006, 1 U.S. dollar equaled 522 colones.

Costa Rica imports oil and coal, but it does not use them for electricity. Instead, it gets most of its power from dams on its rivers that produce huge amounts of hydroelectric power. In the country's volcanic regions, underground steam is harnessed to make electricity. This provides about 10 percent of Costa Rica's energy.

The Five-Colón Note

One of the most beautiful examples of paper money is Costa Rica's five-colón note, which is now out of use. On the reverse side, it reproduced a painting from San José's National Theater. The painting tells the story of coffee, from harvest to export. Women picking beans are dressed in traditional colorful skirts and large straw hats. Men are carrying bags loaded with beans onto ships waiting in the harbor. And, as a reminder that Costa Rica has other crops, a man stands at the center of the painting holding a large bunch of bananas.

Guides carrying telescopes prepare to show tourists the colorful creatures in Manuel Antonio National Park. Tourism is now Costa Rica's leading industry.

Tourism

In 2004, service industries employed almost two-thirds of Costa Rica's workers. Service workers include people employed in government, banking, and tourism.

Tourism has been skyrocketing in recent years. In 1990, 435,000 tourists visited Costa Rica. By 2004, the number had increased to 1.4 million. People come from all over to visit the country's national parks and reserves. They flock to see the Irazú and Poás volcanoes, the spectacular Orosi Valley, and the ruins of the colonial church at Ujarrás. The Pacific beaches of Guanacaste and Puntarenas provinces are also popular.

International Trade

Almost half of Costa Rica's exports go to the United States. Costa Rican goods are also shipped to the Netherlands, Guatemala, Germany, and Malaysia. The main exports are electronic equipment, bananas, medicine, medical equipment, and textiles.

Over half of Costa Rica's imports come from the United States, with Mexico, Japan, Venezuela, Brazil, and Colombia supplying much of the rest. Costa Rica imports some raw materials used in industry as well as machinery, building materials, and oil.

Costa Rica is a member of the Central American Common Market. In 1994, it signed a free-trade agreement with Mexico. This agreement enables Costa Rica to sell many of its products to Mexico without paying import taxes.

Staying in Touch

Costa Rica enjoys freedom of the press. Because most people speak Spanish and almost everyone can read, newspapers and magazines have large readerships. Of the eight daily newspapers, the two with the greatest distribution are *La Nación* and *Diario*

Ships wait to be unloaded at the port of Limón. It is the busiest port in Costa Rica.

Extra. Each has about 120,000 readers. Other major newspapers include *Al Día, La República,* and *La Prensa Libre*. The *Tico Times* is published weekly in English.

About 98 percent of Costa Ricans have radios, and television is available over about 90 percent of the country. About eight hundred thousand personal computers in Costa Rica are hooked up to the Internet, while about half a million Costa Ricans have cell phones.

Juan Santamaría International Airport near San José is the busiest airport in Central America. Two million passengers pass through the airport every year.

Transportation

Costa Rica has easy and regular contact with the rest of the world. The main international airport is just outside of San José. From there, several international airlines have direct flights to South America, Europe, and other parts of North America. A second international airport is at Liberia in Guanacaste province.

Along its Atlantic and Pacific coasts, Costa Rica has several good ports. Puerto Limón and the Moín terminal on the Atlantic coast are equipped to handle the export of bananas and coffee. Caldera, a port on the Gulf of Nicoya, is the main Pacific port.

San José has a large bus system that makes it easy for people to get around the city.

Costa Rica has an extensive network of highways. Most are unpaved and not in good condition. Heavy rains and the occasional earthquake cause landslides and can soon reduce a road to a series of potholes. In 2001, the government began building four major roads across the country.

Long-distance buses are a good way to get around. They are reliable and inexpensive, if sometimes a little slow. Towns have buses and taxis, and rural areas have local bus services. But many people in the countryside still travel on horseback and sometimes by horse and cart.

End of the Line

The construction of Costa Rica's two main railroads was vital to the country's development. The first railroad linked San José with Puerto Limón in 1890. The second line, from San José to Puntarenas, was completed in 1910. Both lines were closed in 1995. Travel on these railways was slow, but the many stops at lively platforms full of people buying and selling food and trinkets made the trip interesting. A section of the line between Limón and Siquirres was reopened in 1999. It is used mainly by tourists and to transport bananas.

Ticos and Their Traditions

COSTA RICANS LIKE TO CALL THEMSELVES TICOS. SOME say the nickname comes from an old colonial saying, "We are all *hermanticos*." The Spanish word *hermanticos* means "little brothers." This implies that all the people of Costa Rica are equal. It is also possible that the term simply reflects the common use of the word ending *-tico*, which means "little" in Spanish. Costa Ricans tend to use *-tico* and *-ico* at the end of words such as *momentico*, meaning "just a little moment." In other Spanish-speaking countries, people are more likely to say *momentito*.

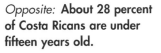
Opposite: **About 28 percent of Costa Ricans are under fifteen years old.**

More than 90 percent of Costa Ricans are of European or mixed European and indigenous backgrounds.

Population of Costa Rica's Largest Cities (2004)	
San José	336,829
Puerto Limón	61,200
Alajuela	47,737
San Francisco	44,628
Desamparados	40,040

Ethnic Costa Rica

About 94 percent of Costa Ricans are either of European descent or are mestizos. Mestizos are people with mixed European and indigenous backgrounds.

Most European immigrants to Costa Rica came from Spain, but others came from Germany, Great Britain, and France. They settled in the highlands and the Meseta Central, and many became successful coffee planters and exporters, merchants, ranchers, and industrialists. Many merged completely into Costa Rican society. Others kept their national identity and traditions by setting up churches and schools in their own language.

The peaceful town of Zarcero lies in the northern Meseta Central. The San Rafael Arcangel Church, which was built in 1895, dominates the town.

Blacks

Blacks are the largest minority group in Costa Rica, making up about 3 percent of the population. They are descendants of the West Indians who arrived to help build the railroad and then stayed to work on the banana plantations in the Caribbean lowlands. The West Indians spoke English and came from islands governed by the United Kingdom. As such, their culture was quite different from that of the Ticos, who at first wanted nothing to do with them.

But in the 1920s, jobs became hard to find in the highlands. Because there were more opportunities on the banana plantations, many Ticos moved to the Caribbean lowlands. This led to friction as the Ticos came to resent the English-speaking blacks and the higher wages they received.

Most black Costa Ricans had ancestors who moved to the country from the Caribbean island of Jamaica. Today, most speak both English and Spanish.

Who Lives in Costa Rica?

Whites and mestizos	94%
Blacks	3%
Chinese	1%
Indigenous people	1%
Other	1%

A hundred years ago, many Costa Ricans of African descent worked on banana plantations. Today, most black Costa Ricans still live in the Caribbean lowlands where the plantations were located.

In the 1930s, disease devastated the Caribbean banana plantations. The United Fruit Company moved its operations to the Pacific coast, but the law did not allow the company to take its black workers along. Many blacks then moved to Panama and the United States to look for work. Others stayed on the Caribbean coast and made a living the best they could by clearing and farming small plots of land in the forest.

The children of the West Indian immigrants were at first not accepted by the Costa Rican government as either Britons or Costa Ricans. This did not change until after the 1948 civil war. Many blacks supported José Figueres Ferrer during the turmoil. Their support was rewarded when a decree was passed ensuring that every person born in Costa Rica had all the rights of Costa Rican citizenship.

Blacks now work in most professions in San José and around the country. In Limón province, many are independent cacao farmers. Others work on the banana plantations.

Indigenous Peoples

Today, indigenous people make up only about 1 percent of Costa Rica's population. The largest groups are the Bribri and the Cabécar. Costa Rica is also home to small groups of Guaymi, Boruca, and Malékus or Guatuso.

The Bribri and Cabécar live on reservations in an isolated part of the Cordillera de Talamanca in southern Costa Rica. Their lifestyle is much the same as that of other poor rural

A Bribri man stands in his doorway. Between thirty thousand and sixty thousand Costa Ricans are indigenous.

people. They grow bananas, corn, beans, fruit, and plants to use for medicines. Their houses are of palm thatch and bamboo, and they generally have some livestock. A small tribe of Bribri, the Kekoldi, breed iguanas. They raise these large lizards until they are full-grown iguanas and then release them into the wild.

The Boruca have more contact with other Costa Ricans. They also have some contact with tourists, since their reservation is not far from a main highway. Some visitors enjoy watching the Boruca craft workers. The women weave clothing and bags, and the men make masks of balsa wood.

The Boruca people are famed for their carved balsa wood masks. About two thousand Borucas live on a reserve in southwestern Costa Rica.

Chorotega Pottery

The Chorotega of Guanacaste province were probably the largest indigenous group in Costa Rica at the time of the Spanish conquest. They were famed for their pottery. Today, in the small town of Guaitíl on the site of an ancient Chorotega community, some women have set up a workshop to produce pots in the old Chorotega style. They use traditional methods and materials to re-create the striking black, red, and white patterns and animal images found on ancient Chorotega pottery. The few surviving Chorotega live on the Matambu reservation near Nicoya, which was once the Chorotega capital.

The Guaymi live along the Costa Rica–Panama border. Guaymi women are known for their long, colorful dresses. They also make attractive textiles and bark-cloth paintings. The paintings combine traditional religious symbols with stylized animals and plants or scenes of daily life. The Guaymi sell these paintings in the local markets and to tourists.

About two thousand Guaymi live in Costa Rica. Many more live farther south in Panama.

For many years, Costa Rican society ignored the nation's indigenous peoples. Then, in the 1960s, following a newspaper campaign highlighting their problems, the National Commission of Indigenous Affairs was created. Its aim was to improve the education, health, nutrition, and community life of the native peoples. Only in 1994 did indigenous Costa Ricans gain the right to vote.

Today, Costa Rica's indigenous people are still the poorest group in the country. The biggest problem they face is that they do not own the land on which they live and work. They are constantly under threat from businesspeople who want to take over land and use it for something else. Some would use it for agriculture. Others would build hotels for tourists. Some reservation land, which had been set aside for use by indigenous people, has already been seized. The native people who lived there received nothing in return.

A Bribri boy from the Talamanca Indigenous Reservation. About three-quarters of indigenous Costa Ricans live in reservation communities.

In recent years, indigenous people have begun to demand a better place in society. In the 1990s, the Bribri and Cabecar founded their own bank. This helps them raise funds to start businesses. Indigenous groups are also using radio to help maintain their identity. Their radio stations are run solely by the local community. Programs cover topics such as agricultural news and education. Most programs are in Spanish, but a few are in indigenous languages.

A Boruca man protests outside the Interamerican Court of Human Rights in San José. His sign reads, "We all have the same rights."

Parts of San José feel much like the United States. Fast food restaurants abound.

Chinese

About 1 percent of Costa Ricans are of Chinese background. Some are the descendants of workers brought in to build the railroad to the Caribbean coast, and others arrived more recently. In San José, the Chinese, or *chinos*, as they are known locally, have been absorbed easily into the urban lifestyle. In small towns, especially in the lowlands, the Chinese own many shops, restaurants, and movie theaters. They also work as traders in the cacao and banana industries.

New Immigrants

Costa Rica has become an attractive destination for Americans interested in retiring somewhere peaceful, safe, and friendly. They have brought some of their northern culture with them. San José now has many American-style fast-food restaurants and bars.

In recent years, the largest number of people arriving in Costa Rica are immigrants from other parts of Latin America. Their arrival has put a great strain on the country's health, education, and social service systems. Today, an estimated 10 to 15 percent of the Costa Rican population is Nicaraguan. Costa Rica is also home to many refugees from Colombia, who have fled war and terrorism.

Language

Spanish is Costa Rica's official language. It is spoken by almost everyone in the country. English, the second most common language in Costa Rica, is now taught in all public schools. Most indigenous languages in Costa Rica have died out. In the Talamanca region, however, some local radio programs and newspaper articles are produced in Bribri. Another language, Maleku, is still spoken by about three hundred people who live on a reservation near Arenal.

A teacher helps a student with reading. About 96 percent of adult Costa Ricans can read and write.

Common Spanish Words and Phrases

Sí	Yes
No	No
Bueno	Good
¿Cómo está usted?	How are you?
Gracias	Thank you
Por favor	Please
¿Qué hora es?	What time is it?
¿Habla inglés?	Do you speak English?
Adiós	Good-bye

Costa Rican Spanish

Compared with the Spanish spoken in other countries, Costa Rican Spanish is quite formal. People speak distinctly, slowly, and without dropping letters at the ends of words. An example of their formality is the use of the word *usted* when speaking to children. Usually in Spanish, children are addressed as *tú*, which is familiar and friendly. In other countries, *usted* is reserved for people one does not know well or for someone who is greatly respected.

Many signs in Costa Rica are in both English and Spanish.

Costa Rican speech is also quite polite. On being introduced to another person, the Costa Rican greeting is *"con mucho gusto"* (kohn MOO-choh GOO-stoh), which means "with much pleasure." This may be followed at the end of the conversation by *"para servirle"* (PAH-ra sayr-VEER-lay), meaning "at your service," or by *"que le vaya bien"* (kay lay VAH-ya BEE-en), meaning "may you go well."

Costa Ricans tend to be friendly and polite to locals and travelers alike.

Costa Ricans also like to call one another by nicknames. Someone who is fat may be called *gordo* (GOR-doh) and a thin person *flaco* (FLA-koh), but no offense is meant—or taken. A common expression that everyone uses to friends and strangers is *mi amor* (MEE a-MOR), meaning "my love." It has no deep significance except that Costa Ricans like to be warm and friendly.

Tiquismos

Some slang words and expressions have crept into Costa Rican Spanish. Ticos call these words *tiquismos,* though several of the words are also used in other countries. Here are some examples:

¡Achará! (ach-a-RAH)	What a pity!
Buena nota (BWAYN-a NOH-ta)	How cool, great ("good grade")
¿Diay? (dee-AH-ee)	Oh dear, but what can you expect?
Maje (MAH-hay) (used by young men)	Buddy, pal
Pura vida (POO-rah VEE-dah)	Great, okay ("pure life")

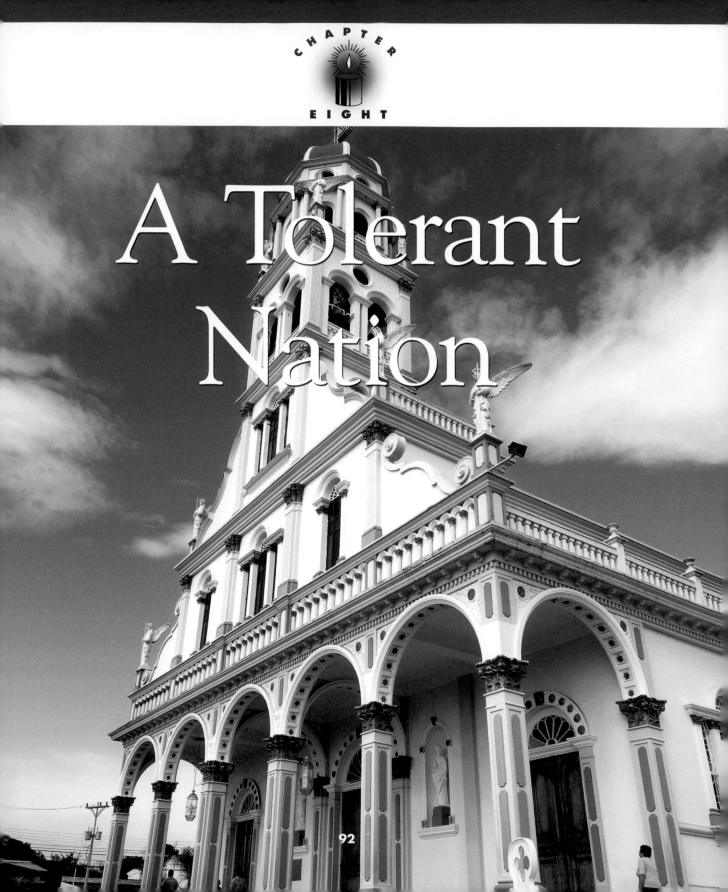

A Tolerant Nation

MOST PEOPLE IN COSTA RICA ARE ROMAN CATHOLIC. Catholicism has been the dominant religion since Spanish missionaries first arrived in the region in the sixteenth century. According to the 1949 constitution, Catholicism is Costa Rica's official religion. But the same constitution allows Costa Ricans to practice whatever religion they choose. Given this freedom of choice, how do the Ticos approach their faiths?

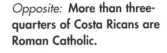

Opposite: **More than three-quarters of Costa Ricans are Roman Catholic.**

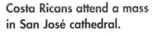

Costa Ricans attend a mass in San José cathedral.

Religions of Costa Rica

Roman Catholic	76%
Evangelical Protestant	14%
Other	7%
None	3%

Seven out ten Ticos call themselves Catholics, but fewer than half are regular churchgoers. Those who do not attend Mass regularly still visit churches for baptisms, weddings, and funerals. At Easter, a few more people go to church, but most take the day as a holiday to visit the countryside or the beach. Still, most homes, offices, and schools have a cross, a shrine, or some kind of religious poster on the wall.

People throng the streets for a procession on Good Friday during the week before Easter. Costa Ricans are most likely to attend religious services around Easter.

While Catholicism is the official religion of Costa Rica, the church is not permitted to be involved in politics. But it is concerned with social conditions. Nuns and priests work among the poor, tending to their physical and spiritual needs while also helping to teach skills that might help families to improve their way of life.

About nine hundred nuns work in Costa Rica.

Indigenous Beliefs

It was not easy for the Spanish missionaries to convert the indigenous peoples of Costa Rica to Christianity. The people of Costa Rica had their own deeply held beliefs that they would not easily give up. These beliefs revolved around the gods and spirits they believed existed in the natural world. The Bribri and Cabécar believed the forest was created by Sibo, who is often depicted as a bird. The native Costa Ricans also had shamans, religious leaders whom they relied on to cure the sick, tell the future, and calm evil spirits.

Other Religions

Protestantism is the second most common religion in Costa Rica. In the past, most Protestant Costa Ricans were from West Indian families living on the Caribbean coast. But in recent years, the number of Protestants in the Meseta Central has increased. Much of this increase is the result of the arrival of evangelical missionaries spreading their beliefs.

A Baptist church in Puerto Viejo. The number of Protestants in Costa Rica has been rising rapidly in recent years.

The growing groups include the Assemblies of God, Jehovah's Witnesses, Seventh-Day Adventists, and many smaller churches. The Church of Jesus Christ of Latter-day Saints, whose followers are often known as Mormans, is well established. The Mormon temple in San José is the regional worship center for Costa Rica and the neighboring countries of Nicaragua, Panama, and Honduras.

Young Costa Ricans worship at a National Day for Prayer celebration in San José, Costa Rica.

A group of American Quakers arrived in Costa Rica in 1951. Most Quakers are pacifists, meaning they do not believe in war. This group of Quakers moved to Costa Rica to protest the military draft that was happening in the United States at the time. They settled in the Cordillera de Tilarán, where they founded a farming community now known as Monteverde.

Costa Rica's First Protestants

William Le Lacheur, who took the first cargo of coffee beans from Costa Rica to England, was probably also the first person to give out Bibles in Costa Rica. Le Lacheur, his son John, and his friend Dr. Richard Brealey began the first Protestant religious services in the country. Brealey held services in his home for seventeen years.

In 1864, Costa Rican Protestants decided they needed their own church. The following year, the iron pieces to build a church were brought from England on one of Le Lacheur's ships. The Church of the Good Shepherd was put up in San José. Today, plaques in the church honor the work of Le Lacheur and Brealey in establishing Protestantism in Costa Rica.

Just an hour north of the city, Poás Volcano attracts many San José residents on Saint Joseph's Day.

Costa Rica is also home to people of other faiths, including Islam, Baha'i, and Judaism. The first Jews in Costa Rica arrived from eastern Europe in the late 1920s. Nearly half came from two villages in Poland. This may explain why Costa Ricans call Jews *polacos* ("Polish"). There are an estimated 2,000 Jews in Costa Rica, and they have their own school in San José with about 350 students.

Religious Festivals

Many villages and towns are named after saints, people whom the Catholic Church believes to be especially holy. The capital, San José, is named after Saint Joseph. On Saint Joseph's feast day, March 19, many people in San José take a holiday. Some join religious processions, while others follow an old tradition and visit Poás Volcano.

The greatest procession in Costa Rica is held to celebrate the Feast of Our Lady of the Angels on August 2 at the massive church in Cartago. This event got its start back on August 2, 1635, when a poor woman, Juana Pereira, was gathering firewood near Cartago. She supposedly discovered a small image of Mary, Jesus's mother, sitting beside a path. Juana took the image home, but it disappeared and was soon rediscovered by

People line up outside the church in Cartago during the Feast of Our Lady of the Angels.

the path. This is said to have happened five times. People in the area felt that the image had special powers, so they built a shrine on the spot where it was found. The poor and the sick soon began making special trips to the shrine to pray for help.

The image is known as *La Negrita* or "the Little Black One," because it is carved on dark stone. It is tiny, only about 3 inches high (8 centimeters). Each August, a million and a half people come to Cartago to pray before La Negrita.

Pilgrims splash themselves with water from a spring at the Church of Our Lady of the Angels in Cartago. They believe the water will protect or heal them.

People prepare floats for a Christmas parade in San José.

Christmas

Although Costa Ricans are not a strongly religious people, they do celebrate religious holidays such as Christmas and Easter. Christmas in Costa Rica is celebrated in much the same way as it is in Europe and the United States. Preparation starts weeks beforehand with decorated Christmas trees, colored lights, and shops filled with gifts. Santa Claus is often seen dressed in his red suit and sporting a bushy white beard. In San José during Christmas week, fireworks, bullfights, and fairs add to the excitement.

On Christmas Eve, families and friends gather to eat turkey and corn tamales. Children are usually eager to get to bed, anticipating what Santa Claus will bring. Many families continue with the festivities until the New Year.

Culture and Customs

In 1970, President José Figueres Ferrer created the Ministry of Culture, Youth, and Sports. This breathed new life into Costa Rican arts, especially music. Before that time, the National Symphony Orchestra gave just a few concerts each year. But after 1970, the orchestra was revitalized. By 1978, the orchestra was performing at the White House in Washington, D.C.

Founded in 1988, the Coro Surá was the first professional choir in Central America. The choir takes its name from a Costa Rican tree, the surá. Symbolically, each member of the choir represents a branch of the tree.

Opposite: **Costa Rica's top singers and musicians perform at the National Theater in San José.**

The National Theater opened in 1897. It was Costa Rica's first world-class concert hall.

The Castella Conservatory in San José is one of the top venues for musical performances. The National Theater is also in the capital, and theater groups perform at both the University of Costa Rica and the National University.

Dance

Few traditional folk dances have survived in Costa Rica, but the best known come from Guanacaste province. The most

Many folk dances are performed to the music of the marimba, a large wooden xylophone. Three or four people often play a marimba at one time.

popular is the Punto Guanacaste. Couples perform a foot stomping dance to music played on the guitar and a kind of xylophone called the marimba.

Folk dancing in Costa Rica is a blur of colorful skirts and handkerchiefs.

On the Caribbean coast, festivals sometimes feature traditional maypole dances. Colored ribbons are tied to the top of a pole. The dancers weave in and out, so that the ribbons fold over one another down the length of the pole. Drums and banjos provide rhythmic music.

Many young Costa Ricans enjoy spending Saturday night at the local dance hall. They dance for hours to Latin music such as the salsa and the lambada, and to Caribbean rhythms. Rock and swing music are also popular.

The Jade Museum

On the eleventh floor of an ordinary-looking office building in downtown San José is the Jade Museum. Though the outside of the building does not look like much, inside is the world's largest collection of American jade. A staggering number of jade artifacts carved by ancient Costa Ricans are on display.

Since Costa Rica has no known source of jade, most experts assume that the jade was brought in from what is now Guatemala. Many of the jade objects are carved axe heads depicting a freakish human or animal. The animals include jaguars, monkeys, birds, reptiles, and a double-headed crocodile.

The museum also displays gold artifacts such as headbands and earrings. Pottery on display at the museum ranges from a period of about 300 B.C. to A.D. 1550. It includes bowls, jars, and three-legged tables used for grinding corn. The museum also displays ceramic figurines, many intricately decorated with animals and weird human faces.

Costa Rican art only came into its own in the late 1920s, with artists such as Teodorico Quirós (1897–1977) and Francisco Amighetti (1907–) in the lead. Searching for a Costa Rican national identity, they depicted local scenes, particularly rural landscapes, homes, and people. Sculptors drew on the local environment and on early indigenous art. Costa Rica's best-known sculptor was Francisco "Paco" Zuñiga (1912–1998). He is famous for his strong, serene female figures.

Sculptor Francisco Zuñiga first studied art in San José. He then moved to Mexico City, where he spent most of his career.

Isidro Con Wong is one of Costa Rica's best-known contemporary artists. Con was born in 1931 to Chinese immigrant parents. He spent the first part of his adult life working on the land and has been strongly influenced by the environment. His paintings are colorful and magical. They often feature mountains, moons, and bulls. Typically, tiny bulls sit on the branches of a tree below a full moon in a dark blue sky that is full of twinkling lights. Another renowned contemporary artist is Luis Chacón, who uses intense colors and strong lines. Ana Griselda Hine and Gioconda Rojas Howell are two of Costa Rica's foremost women artists.

Francisco Amighetti

Francisco Amighetti is Costa Rica's best-known artist. Born to an Italian immigrant in 1907, he became an engraver, graphic artist, painter, and teacher, and his work spanned much of the twentieth century. He went to school in San José and studied art at the Academia de Bellas Artes. Many of his wood engravings and paintings depict ordinary people in everyday activities. They reflect life as it is in Costa Rica.

Amighetti traveled a great deal in Mexico and South and Central America. Influences from these places appear in his work. For example, murals—large paintings on walls—are an important art form in Mexico. Amighetti introduced mural painting to Costa Rica. He also wrote several books about his travels.

Costa Rica's most famous folk art is its brightly painted oxcarts. Early in the twentieth century, the wife of Fructuoso Barrantes, a cart maker, decided to brighten her husband's carts with colorful geometric designs. The idea caught on. Soon flowers, leaves, vegetables, and even landscapes were being painted on oxcarts. Today, the carts are often displayed in local festivals, and toy oxcarts are sold to tourists. Other popular Costa Rican crafts include wooden bowls and trays, woven baskets and mats, and leather goods.

When Costa Ricans began painting oxcarts, they used a lot of greens and gray. Today, orange and blue are more common.

Literature

Costa Rican writers have generally focused on the political and social scene around them. Joaquín García Monge (1881–1958) wrote the first important Costa Rican novel, *El Moto*. He was also the longtime editor of *El Repertorio Americano*, a magazine widely acclaimed for its essays. In the 1930s and 1940s, many novels concerned landlords exploiting the poor. *Mamita Yunái*, written by Carlos Luis Fallas about the plight of the banana workers, is one of the best. More recent leading writers include the poet and essayist Alfonso Chase, who was awarded the 2000 Magón Award, Costa Rica's major culture prize.

Sports

Costa Ricans are passionate about soccer, or *fútbol*, as they call it. Matches are played regularly in San José's Saprissa Stadium in front of large crowds. From an early age, young children kick a ball around on any spare patch of ground. Adults do much the same when they are not working.

Other sports enjoyed in Costa Rica include basketball, volleyball, baseball, and tennis. The wealthy enjoy golf and polo. Pool is also popular. The Meseta Central is good country for horseback riding.

As if all this were not enough, Costa Rica is a marvelous place for water sports. The sea fishing is excellent. And for many, swimming at uncrowded beaches offers the best opportunity to relax. Costa Rica has some of the best surfing waves in the world. Lake Arenal, which is considered one of the world's top spots for windsurfing, has steady winds from December to April. The coast also has places to windsurf. Some people prefer scuba diving among schools of exotic fish. White-water rafting and kayaking have become popular in Costa Rica. The excellent conditions on some of Costa Rica's rivers attract international competitors and many tourists.

Soccer is by far the most popular sport in Costa Rica.

Gold!

Swimmer Claudia Poll Ahrens was the first Costa Rican to win a gold medal in the Olympic Games. In 1996, she took home the gold in the 200-meter freestyle swim. Poll was born in Managua, Nicaragua, in 1972. Her family moved to Costa Rica when she was very young. Poll grew up to be 6 foot 5 inches (196 cm) tall and extremely strong. She broke three world records in the 1990s and took home two bronze medals in the 2000 Olympics. Her older sister Sylvia was also a world-class swimmer. She won Costa Rica's first-ever Olympic medal, taking home a silver in the 1988 Games.

Celebrating Together

Costa Ricans enjoy numerous national holidays. For many families, the holidays provide a chance to spend time in the countryside, walking or hiking in the mountains or simply relaxing on the beach.

For important holidays such as Easter and Christmas, the whole country shuts down. Banks, post offices, museums, and

---

Columbus Day in Puerto Limón

The biggest party of the year in Puerto Limón takes place the week before Columbus Day, the anniversary of the day Columbus first arrived in the Americas. During this week, called Carnaval, Puerto Limón is packed with Costa Ricans from every part of the country, as well as foreign tourists. The most spectacular event of the week is a parade of floats with people dressed in bright African-Caribbean costumes.

Other events include fireworks displays, theater, and bull running.

But the heart of Carnaval is the music. Puerto Limón throbs to the sound of African-Caribbean music played on tambourines, drums, and whistles. Every corner of the town seems to be alive with live bands or blasting sound systems. The center of the action is near the port. There, people dance the night away.

government offices close, usually for an entire week. Even for a local festival in the provinces, everything shuts for several days.

Towns and villages throughout Costa Rica hold their own fairs. These are opportunities for the whole community to get together and have some fun. Entertainment often includes fair rides and bingo, beauty contests and bullfighting. Children love the fireworks, adults wear themselves out from dancing, and everyone gets their fill from stalls piled high with food and drink.

Festival of the Little Devils

Many places in Central and South America hold festivals that reenact the Spanish conquest. In Costa Rica, the Boruca people celebrate the *Fiesta de los Diablitos,* the "Festival of the Little Devils," for three days over the New Year.

A man from the village plays the part of a bull—he represents the Spaniards—and other villagers become "devils." They disguise themselves with homemade masks. At midnight on December 30, the devils and musicians playing pipes, drums, and guitars meet at the top of a hill. During that night and for the next three days, they taunt the "bull," while moving from house to house to receive food and drink. Eventually, the "bull" is killed. This brings a different ending to the story of the Spanish conquest, for in the Fiesta de los Diablitos, the native people conquer the Spaniards!

Everyday Life

ALL OVER THE WORLD, PEOPLE ARE MOVING FROM rural to urban areas. The reason is simple: cities and towns usually offer better schools and medical care. But in Costa Rica, the population remains fairly evenly split between towns and the countryside. However, people are not evenly spread around the country. More than half of Costa Ricans live on the Meseta Central, while few live in the vast lowlands on the Caribbean coast.

Costa Ricans will tell you that they remain in rural areas because their roots are in the land. In many ways, family life is more important to Costa Ricans than the benefits of city life. Family loyalty is strong, and in rural areas, families help one another in the house and on the farm. Even so, many people have taken their chances and set up a home on the outskirts of San José or another city.

Opposite: **Most school-children in Costa Rica wear uniforms.**

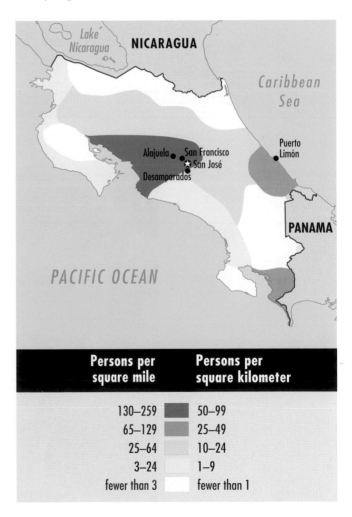

Persons per square mile	Persons per square kilometer
130–259	50–99
65–129	25–49
25–64	10–24
3–24	1–9
fewer than 3	fewer than 1

Housing

How Costa Rican houses are built depends on where they are located.

On the Meseta Central, most working people live in houses built of concrete blocks or bricks with tile or corrugated iron roofs. Many are just one story, and most are painted in bright colors. Inside, the main room, called the *sala*, usually has a couch and chairs, a central table, and several pictures or posters on the walls. The other rooms in the house are the kitchen, maybe a dining room, a bathroom, and two or three bedrooms.

Older houses on the Meseta Central, and those in more remote areas, are built of adobe mud bricks with a roof of clay tiles. Some have verandas overlooking central patios. In rural areas, porches and roofs are often covered with flowers, ferns, and other greenery.

A country house in the Meseta Central is covered with greenery.

Homes in the coastal lowlands are generally built of wood. They stand on stilts to protect the house from flooding and to keep out wild animals. The shaded space under the floor can be used as a work area and for drying clothes. Many houses in the lowlands have shutters rather than windows so that air can flow through. They also have balconies where families and friends can sit and chat in the warm evenings.

Most Costa Rican houses have running water and electricity. But this is not true in the slums on the outskirts of San José and other towns. The homes there are very simple. They are made of wood, cardboard, corrugated iron, or whatever else people can find.

The houses of the wealthy in Costa Rica are often surrounded by high concrete walls to keep out burglars. These houses are similar to houses in the United States or Europe, with garages, paved driveways, and sometimes swimming pools.

Some neighborhoods in San José are filled with ramshackle buildings. About 10 percent of the people in Costa Rica live on less than two dollars a day.

Costa Rica has a strong commitment to health care. All medical students spend part of their training working in rural areas.

Health and Poverty

In the past twenty years, the poverty rate in Costa Rica has dropped from 40 percent to under 20 percent. Family size affects poverty, and that, too, has been dropping steadily over the decades. Today, many parents have only two or three children, though they may have come from families with eight or nine children. Their grandparents quite possibly had twelve or fourteen siblings. Poor and rural Costa Ricans tend to have larger families however.

Improving health is also important in reducing poverty. To be healthy, people need clean water and nutritious food, and in recent years, the Costa Rican government has worked hard to improve both. In 2002, 97 percent of Costa Ricans had access to safe water.

Costa Rica has one of the most generous social welfare programs in Central America. The government gives financial help to working people who suffer an injury, to the sick, and to women taking time off work to care for new babies. Workers are also entitled to old-age pensions, and the disabled receive help as well.

The government is taking steps to improve nutrition. Inadequate food was, for many years, an important reason why so many Costa Rican children died young. In the 1970s, a rural health program was begun to provide meals for young children, pregnant women, and nursing mothers. The program also set up medical offices in rural communities that

Medicinal herbs are for sale at markets throughout Costa Rica.

doctors and nurses visit on a regular basis. Vaccinations, medicine, and health care for pregnant mothers are provided to help reduce disease. Despite these efforts, deadly diseases such as dysentery and typhoid remain a problem in some areas.

Costa Rica's best hospitals and medical treatment are in San José. Many Costa Ricans also have great faith in herbal medicines. Stands of dried plants and herbs to be used as medicines are found in many markets.

Espaleta

Many children in Costa Rica learn to ride horses at a very early age. One popular game—*espaleta*—requires excellent horsemanship. In espaleta, each competitor races on horseback down a track while holding a small metal lance. The object of the game is to stick the lance through a ring that is suspended from a rope at the end of the path. The problem is that the ring is only slightly larger than a wedding ring. The winner is the person who passes the lance through the ring the most times.

Education

Costa Rica has long shown a commitment to education. As early as 1869, Costa Rican law said that all children must attend school and that schooling should be free. Between 1885 and 1888, Minister of Education Mauro Fernández opened many schools and provided textbooks. Large sums of money from the coffee industry helped him succeed. In about

Students line up during an assembly in Tortuguero. More than 90 percent of Costa Rican children finish elementary school.

About half of young people in Costa Rica attend high school.

thirty years, the number of people who were unable to read or write dropped from about 75 percent to 25 percent of the population. Today, just 4 percent of adult Costa Ricans cannot read or write.

Costa Rican children attend school from age six until they are at least fifteen years old. They spend six years at primary level and three years at secondary level. Students may then concentrate on just two or three subjects for another two years before deciding whether to attend college. Costa Rican children study Spanish and English, social studies, math, sciences, music, religion, arts, physical education, and theater studies. The school year begins in March and ends in November.

Costa Rica's National Holidays

New Year's Day	January 1
Saint Joseph's Day	March 19
Ash Wednesday	February or March
Holy Week	March or April
Juan Santamaría Day	April 11
Labor Day	May 1
Feast of Our Lady of the Angels	August 2
Feast of the Assumption and Mother's Day	August 15
Independence Day	September 15
Columbus Day	October 12
All Souls' Day	November 2
Christmas Day	December 25

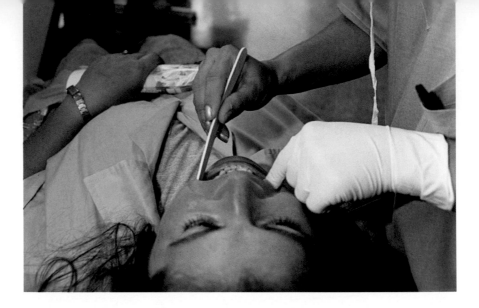

Students at the Latin American University of Science and Technology can study dentistry.

Costa Rica is the site of four public universities and several private ones. The largest is the University of Costa Rica, which has thirty-five thousand students. The school began in 1940, with departments of law, fine arts, agriculture, pharmacy, and education. Other departments, including dentistry and journalism, have since been added.

Spaceman

Franklin Chang-Díaz was the first astronaut to come from Latin America. He was born in San José in April 1950. His father was a Costa Rican of Chinese descent. Chang-Díaz attended school in San José, finished high school in the United States, and earned a bachelor of science degree in mechanical engineering from the University of Connecticut in 1973. He went on to get his doctorate and in 1977 became a U.S. citizen. He was accepted by NASA to train as an astronaut in 1980 and in 1986 made his first space mission, aboard the *Columbia* space shuttle. Chang-Díaz retired from NASA in 2005. By that time, he had traveled into space seven times, logging more than 1,601 hours in space, including 19 hours and 31 minutes in three spacewalks.

Costa Rican food tends to be simple but tasty. A typical Costa Rican breakfast is *gallo pinto*, which many people regard as the country's national dish. *Gallo pinto* means "painted rooster," but the name has little relation to the dish. Gallo pinto is a mixture of red and white beans, white rice, onions, peppers, and seasonings. Sometimes it is served with scrambled eggs.

Beans and rice are the basics of many Costa Rican dishes. Perhaps the best known is *casado*, a dish that includes stewed beef or fish, fried plantains, cabbage or coleslaw, and rice and beans.

Most Costa Rican food comes with rice and beans.

Soups and stews are common in Costa Rica. *Olla de carne* consists of beef, plantains, corn, yucca, ñampi, and chayote, which are local vegetables. *Sopa negra*, a black bean soup with a poached egg, and *picadillo*, a meat and vegetable stew, are also favorites.

The most popular fish dish in Costa Rica is *ceviche*. It consists of raw fish that has been prepared in lime juice with onion, garlic, and cilantro.

Popular snacks include *arreglados*, bread filled with meat and vegetables; and *empanadas*, small pastry pies with similar fillings. *Pan de yuca*, or yucca bread, is a specialty sold in street markets.

Many tasty treats can be bought on the streets of Costa Rica. Here, a woman sells empanadas at a stand in Limón.

Caribbean Cooking

The food prepared in the Caribbean lowlands is different from that eaten in the highlands. Caribbean cooking uses more spices, including coriander, cumin, paprika, cloves, and chilies. The other secret is coconut milk, which can turn an average dish of rice and beans into a delicious meal. Coconut milk is not the liquid inside a coconut. Instead, it is obtained by grating the meat of the coconut and then pressing it. Coconut milk is the vital ingredient in a dish called *rundown*. Rundown is a vegetable stew made with meat or fish, plantains, and breadfruit. The best rundown is cooked for many hours.

Costa Ricans love sweet puddings and cakes, and a favorite in the Caribbean lowlands is *pan bon*, a sweet, sticky bun glazed with cheese and fruit.

A Feast of Fruits

Many kinds of fruits are grown in Costa Rica, including bananas, pineapples, papayas, mangoes, passion fruits, melons, and lemons. Less-familiar fruits include:

pejbaye—small green or orange palm fruit widely used in cooking; it is related to the coconut.

mamónes chino—small red or yellow fruit with a spiny skin and fleshy fruit; they are often sold by the dozen on street corners.

anono—custard apple; fruit with the taste of custard.

carambolá—star fruit; when the fruit is cut, it has the shape of a star.

marañón—its seed is the cashew nut.

guanabana—a dark green prickly fruit that tastes something like strawberry or pineapple.

tamarindo—the fruit of the tamarind tree; the sticky pulp that surrounds the seeds is used as a flavoring, particularly in drinks.

Tortillas are sometimes cooked over open fires. They are served with almost every meal.

Guanacaste Gourmet

Guanacaste cooking is distinctive for its use of corn, the most widely grown crop among the native peoples who once were the only people in the region. Corn is the basis of tortillas, the thin, floury pancakes eaten almost everywhere in Central America and Mexico. Usually they are filled with meat, chicken, or cheese. *Chorreados*, another kind of pancake, are generally served with *natilla*, which is like sour cream. Tamales, which the Chorotega made hundreds of years ago, are still a favorite festival food. They are made from cornmeal dough mixed with a variety of fillings, wrapped in banana leaves, and boiled.

In Guanacaste, anyone looking for a quick snack should try *tanelas* or *rosquillas*. One traveler described them as tasting like a combination of tortillas and doughnuts! Favorite corn-based drinks include *horchata*, which is spiced with cinnamon, and *pinolillo*, made with roasted corn.

Alajuela is one of Costa Rica's leading coffee-growing regions. The local coffee is renowned for its bold flavor.

The Golden Bean

The most popular drink in Costa Rica is, of course, coffee. It is now well over 150 years since the crop was first grown in the Meseta Central. For a time, it was Costa Rica's major export and brought hope and wealth to a society that a hundred years earlier was the poorest in Central America. Coffee has funded much of the country's development—its roads, bridges, schools, hospitals, railroads, and many public buildings. And coffee barons have become presidents! No wonder it is known as *el grano d'oro*, "the golden bean."

Timeline

Costa Rica History

Early people begin farming in what is now Costa Rica — **ca. 2000** B.C.

The Chorotega people arrive in Costa Rica from what is now Mexico. — A.D. **1300s**

Christopher Columbus arrives in Costa Rica. — 1502

Juan Vásquez de Coronado founds the first permanent European settlement, at Cartago. — 1564

Mexico, Costa Rica, and other Central American territories gain independence from Spain. — 1821

The United Provinces of Central America is formed — 1823

World History

2500 B.C. — Egyptians build the pyramids and the Sphinx in Giza.

563 B.C. — The Buddha is born in India.

A.D. **313** — The Roman emperor Constantine legalizes Christianity.

610 — The Prophet Muhammad begins preaching a new religion called Islam.

1054 — The Eastern (Orthodox) and Western (Roman Catholic) Churches break apart.

1095 — The Crusades begin.

1215 — King John seals the Magna Carta.

1300s — The Renaissance begins in Italy.

1347 — The plague sweeps through Europe.

1453 — Ottoman Turks capture Constantinople, conquering the Byzantine Empire.

1492 — Columbus arrives in North America.

1500s — Reformers break away from the Catholic Church, and Protestantism is born.

1776 — The Declaration of Independence is signed.

1789 — The French Revolution begins.

Costa Rica History

The United Provinces of Central America breaks apart.	1840
The first shipment of Costa Rican coffee is sent to England.	1843
William Walker invades Costa Rica.	1856
General Tomás Guardia overthrows the government of Costa Rica.	1870
A railroad is built connecting San José and Puerto Limón.	1872–1890
José Joaquín Rodríguez is elected president in the first truly democratic elections in Central America.	1890
The worst earthquake in Costa Rican history kills 1,750 people.	1910
Rafael Ángel Calderón Guardia becomes president and begins social reforms	1940
Civil war engulfs Costa Rica.	1948
Costa Rica's present constitution is enacted.	1949
Arenal Volcano erupts, killing 78 people.	1968
President Oscar Arias Sánchez wins the Nobel Peace Prize.	1987
Indigenous Costa Ricans gain the right to vote.	1994
Oscar Arias Sánchez is again elected president.	2006

World History

1865	The American Civil War ends.
1879	The first practical light bulb is invented.
1914	World War I breaks out.
1917	The Bolshevik Revolution brings communism to Russia.
1929	A worldwide economic depression begins.
1939	World War II begins.
1945	World War II ends.
1957	The Vietnam War starts.
1969	Humans land on the Moon.
1975	The Vietnam War ends.
1989	The Berlin Wall is torn down as communism crumbles in Eastern Europe.
1991	The Soviet Union breaks into separate states.
2001	Terrorists attack the World Trade Center, New York, and the Pentagon, Washington, D.C.

Fast Facts

Official name: Republic of Costa Rica

Capital: San José

Official language: Spanish

San José

Costa Rica's flag

Nicoya Peninsula

Official religion:	None	
National anthem:	"Noble Patria, Tu Hermosa Bandera" ("Noble Homeland, Your Beautiful Flag")	
Government:	Multiparty republic	
Head of government:	President	
Area:	19,730 square miles (51,100 sq km)	
Latitude and longitude of geographic center:	10°0'N, 84°0'W	
Bordering countries	Nicaragua to the north, Panama to the south	
Highest elevation:	Chirripó Grande, 12,530 feet (3,819 m)	
Lowest elevation:	Sea level, along the coasts	

Average high temperature:

	June	December
San José	79°F (26°C)	75°F (24°C)
Puerto Limón	85°F (29°C)	83°F (28°C)

Average low temperature:

	June	December
San José	62°F (17°C)	58°F (14°C)
Puerto Limón	75°F (24°C)	72°F (22°C)

Average annual precipitation	100 inches (254 cm)	
Average precipitation extremes:	128 inches (325 cm) of rainfall on the east coast; 14 inches (36 cm) of rainfall in the southwest	
National population (2004 est.):	4,075,261	

Monteverde Cloud
Forest Reserve

Currency

Population of largest cities (2004 est):

San José	336,829
Puerto Limón	61,200
Alajuela	47,737
San Francisco	44,628
Desamparados	40,040

Famous landmarks:
- ▶ *Jade Museum,* San José
- ▶ *Church of Our Lady of the Angels,* Cartago
- ▶ *Arenal Volcano,* La Fortuna
- ▶ *Monteverde Cloud Forest Reserve,* Santa Elena
- ▶ *Corcovado National Park,* Osa Peninsula
- ▶ *Chirripó National Park,* San Isidro

Industry: For much of its history, Costa Rica was an agricultural nation, growing primarily bananas and coffee. In recent years, the crops have become more varied, and sugarcane, cacao, and fruits are now also common. Industry replaced agriculture as the most important part of the Costa Rican economy in the 1990s. Today, the manufacture of computer equipment is a leading industry. Businesses have invested in Costa Rica because it is politically stable and has a well-educated population. Tourism has also become central to the nation's economy.

Currency: The colón, which is divided into 100 céntimos. In 2006, 1 U.S. dollar equaled 522 colones.

System of weights and measures: Metric system

Literacy (2003 est.): 96 percent

Elderly Costa Ricans

Oscar Arias Sánchez

Common Spanish words and phrases:

Sí	Yes
No	No.
Bueno	Good
¿Cómo está usted?	How are you?
Gracias	Thank you
Por favor	Please
¿Qué hora es?	What time is it?
¿Habla inglés?	Do you speak English?
Adiós	Good-bye

Famous Costa Ricans:

Francisco Amighetti *Artist*	(1907–)
Oscar Arias Sánchez *President and Nobel Prize winner*	(1941–)
Alfonso Chase *Writer*	(1945–)
José Figueres Ferrer *President*	(1906–1990)
Joaquín García Monge *Writer*	(1881–1958)
Juan Mora Fernández *First president*	(1784–1854)
Claudia Poll Ahrens *Swimmer*	(1972–)
Francisco "Paco" Zuñiga *Sculptor*	(1912–1998)

To Find Out More

Books

▶ Cunningham, Patrick. *Costa Rica*. Letters from around the World series. North Mankato, Minn.: Cherrytree Books, 2004.

▶ Deady, Kathleen W. *Costa Rica*. New York: Children's Press, 2004.

▶ *Into Wild Costa Rica*. San Diego: Blackbirch Press, 2004.

▶ Miller, Debra A. *Costa Rica*. San Diego: Lucent Books, 2005.

▶ Morrison, Marion. *Guide to Costa Rica*. Jackson, Tenn.: Davidson Titles, 2000.

▶ Streissguth, Tom. *Costa Rica in Pictures*. Minneapolis: Lerner, 2005.

Web Sites

▶ **Arenal Volcano Costa Rica**
www.arenal.net
To see spectacular images and hear the sounds of Arenal Volcano erupting.

▶ **Costa Rica National Parks**
http://www.costarica-nationalparks. com
For all kinds of information about Costa Rica's extensive park system.

▶ **The World Factbook: Costa Rica**
www.cia.gov/cia/publications/fact-book/geos/cs.html
For facts and statistics on Costa Rica.

Organizations and Embassies

▶ Embassy of Costa Rica
2114 S Street, NW
Washington, DC 20008
202/234-2943
www.costarica-embassy.org

Index

Page numbers in *italics* indicate illustrations.

industry. *See* manufacturing.
influenza, 41
insect life, 27, 32, 33
Intel Corporation, 71
InterAmerican Court of Human
    Rights, 11, *87*
international parks, *10*, 35, *35*, 130
Internet, 76, 142-143
Irazú volcano, 16, 18, *19*, 21, 42, 63, 74
Isla Bolaños, 23
Isla del Coco, 10, 19, 24
Isla Tortuga, 23, *23*
Islamic religion, 98
islands, 23, *23*

J

Jade Museum, 106, *106*
Jiménez Oreamuno, Ricardo, 48–49, *48*
Joseph (saint), 62, 98–99, 121
Juan Santamaría International
    Airport, 76, *76*
Judaism, 98
judicial branch of government, 56, 58
junta government, 51

K

kayaking, 111
Keith, Minor Cooper, 46-47, *47*
Kekoldi Bribri people, 84
Kennedy, John F., 63

L

La Amistad International Park, *10*,
    35, 130
La Carpintera, 18
La Lucha sin Fin (farm), 51
La Nación newspaper, 75
La Negrita (religious symbol), 100
La Prensa Libre newspaper, 76
La República newspaper, 76
Lake Arenal, 16, 19, *19*, 110–111
lambada music, 105

languages
    Bribri, 89
    English, 89, *90*
    indigenous, 87
    Maleku, 89
    Spanish, 87, 89, 90–91, *90*
    tiquismos (slang words), 91
Lankester, Charles, 21
Lankester Gardens, 21
Latin American University of Science
    and Technology, *122*
Le Lacheur, John, 97
Le Lacheur, William, 44, 97
Legislative Assembly, 57–58
legislative branch of government, 56,
    57–58
Liberia, *10*, 76
Limón province, 58, *75*, 83, *124*
literacy rate, 89
literature, 110
livestock, 12, 20, 22, 30, 41, 69, 70, *70*, 84
local governments. *See* provincial
    governments.

M

Magón Award, 110
malaria, 46
Maleku language, 89
Maléku people, 83
Mamita Yunái (Carlos Luis Fallas), 110
mamónes chino (fruit), 125
manatees, 35
Manuel Antonio National Park, *74*
manufacturing, 65, 67, 71–72
maps. *See also* historical maps.
    geopolitical, *10*
    population density, *115*
    resources, *70*
    San José, *63*
    topographical, *19*
marañón (fruit), 125
margay cats, *31*
Maria Gutiérrez, Manuel, 60

María Zeledón, José, 60
marimba (musical instrument), *104*, 105
marine life, 35, 70
maypole dances, 105
Meseta Central, 20, *20*, 24, 40, 65, 67,
    80, *80*, 96, 110, 115, 116, *116*, 127
military, 9
mining, 13, 72–73
Ministry of Culture, Youth, and
    Sports, 103
Miskito people, 41, 42
missionaries, 93, 96
Moín terminal, 76
monkeys, 26, *27*, 28, *31*, 32, 34, *106*
Monteverde Cloud Forest Reserve,
    10, 13, *33*, 33, 97, 132, *132*
Mora Fernández, Juan, 43, 133
Mora, Juan Rafael, 45
music, 60, 103, *103*, 104, *104*, 105,
    112, 113, 121

N

natilla (cream), 126
national anthem, 60
National Assembly, 50-51
national bird, 28, *28*
National Commission of Indigenous
    Affairs, 85
national dish, 123
national flag, 59, *59*
national flower, 33, *33*
national holidays, 112–113, 121
National Liberation Party, 50–51
national parks, *10*, 12–13, 24, 29–30, *31*,
    32, 34, 35, *35*, 74, *74*, 130, 132, 135
National Symphony Orchestra, 103
National Theater, *73*, *102*, *103*, 104
national tree, 30, *30*
natural resources map, *70*
nature reserves, 12–13
Nicaragua, *10*, 15, *19*, 22, 23, 39, *39*,
    41, 43, 45, 52, 53, 61, *70*, 88, 97,
    112, *115*

Meet the Author

F ROM THE MOMENT MARION MORRISON SET FOOT IN LATIN America soon after she graduated from the University of Wales, she felt at home with the region and its people. "At the time, I had no idea that my life would become so firmly tied to their way of life, history, and enormously varied cultures," she says. Since then, Marion and her husband, Tony, have traveled extensively in Latin America, making television documentaries, writing books, and contributing to newspapers and magazines.

"Costa Rica is tiny and quite extraordinary," says Marion. In preparing for this book, she relied on her own experience and that of her friends, including the photographers who contribute to the picture library she runs from her home in Britain. "Sometimes Costa Rica makes our daily mainstream news with a volcanic eruption, but largely life continues there unobtrusively. Fortunately, the Internet keeps me up-to-date with daily affairs, and I am able to be in touch with friends."

She has found the Internet to be an extremely helpful research tool. "It has greater depths the more you use it," says Marion, "and even more information is added daily. I find my knowledge of Spanish has helped, as these days the Costa Ricans themselves are adding items about their country, the politics, the natural history, and environmental concerns."

Marion has written many other books for the Enchantment of the World series. She continues to travel, sometimes to places new to her, often stopping along the way to meet friends or contacts made via e-mail or telephone. "Nothing can make a livelier discussion than meeting other followers of life in Latin America," she says.

Photo Credits

Photographs © 2007:

age fotostock: 9, 14, 80, 92, 131 bottom (Jon Arnold), 62, 130 (Alvaro Leiva), 74, 76, 93 (Doug Scott)

Alamy Images: 111 (Bill Bachmann), 63 (John Coletti/Jon Arnold Images), 22, 70 (Danita Delimont), 86 (Robert Fried), 126 (Roberto Soncin Gerometta), 30 (Guillen Photography), 25 (Zach Holmes), 64 (James Davis Photography), 79 (Huw Jones), 101 (Mark Pearson), 47 (Popperfoto), 83 (David South), 32 (Corey Wise), 18 (Woodfall Wild Images)

AP/Wide World Photos: 59 bottom (Esteban Felix), 61 (Greg Gibson), 36, 95, 97, 98, 105 (Kent Gilbert)

Art Directors and TRIP Photo Library: 72 (Les Hannah), 88 (Andria Massey), 23 (Darren Maybury)

Art Resource, NY/Museo Nacional de Arte Moderno, Mexico City, D.F., Mexico: 107

Bridgeman Art Library International Ltd., London/New York/British Museum, London, UK: 7 bottom, 37

Corbis Images: 16 (Jeffery Arguedas/epa), 44, 49, 50, 51 (Bettmann), 7 top, 12 (Gary Braasch), 54 (Jan Butchofsky-Houser), 90 (Ralph Clevenger), 15, 27 (Michael & Patricia Fogden), cover, 6, 13, 114 (Blaine Harrington III), 104 (Kit Kittle), 91, 133 top (Bob Krist), 65, 102 (Danny Lehman), 11 (Craig Lovell), 21 top (Stephanie Maze), 75, 94, 100, 120, 124 (Martin Rogers), 29 (Kevin Schafer), 28 top (Roger Tidman), 122 bottom (Frank Trapper/Sygma), 41, 68, 84, 87, 99, 113 (Juan Carlos Ulate/Reuters), 82 (Underwood & Underwood), 40, 46

Danita Delimont Stock Photography: 77 (Jon Arnold), 109 (Jeff Greenberg), 123 (Cindy Miller Hopkins)

Dembinsky Photo Assoc./Jim Battles: 89

Envision Stock Photography Inc./Steven Pace: 69

Getty Images: 118, 122 top (Teresita Chavarria/AFP), 81 (Steve Dunwell/ The Image Bank), 57, 133 bottom (Jeff Haynes/AFP), 127 (Chase Jarvis/The Image Bank), 33 bottom, 132 top (Frans Lemmens/Iconica), 56 (Mayela Lopez/ AFP), 71 (Gilles Mingasson), 48 (Roger Viollet Collection)

Index Stock Imagery: 73 top, 121, 132 bottom (Hirb), 8 (Travel Ink Photo Library)

Kevin Schafer: 28 bottom, 35

Landov, LLC/Reuters: 55 (Tomas Bravo), 112 (Kai Pfaffenbach)

Lonely Planet Images: 106 (Christopher P. Baker), 21 bottom (Christer Fredriksson), 26 (Ralph Lee Hopkins)

MapQuest.com, Inc.: 59 top, 131 top

Marco Saborio: 85 bottom, 108

Masterfile/Alberto Biscaro: 2, 103

Minden Pictures: 31 (Gerry Ellis), 33 top (Michael & Patricia Fogden), 24 (Flip Nicklin)

Seapics.com/Doug Perrine: 34

South American Pictures: 38, 116 (Jevan Berrange), 96 (Britt Dyer), 66 (Robert Francis), 117, 119 (Robert Francis), 73 bottom

The Image Works: 20 (Mario Algaze), 78 (Bill Bachmann), 53 (Charles Bonnay), 85 top (James Marshall), 42, 45 (Mary Evans Picture Library)

Maps and Illustrations by XNR Productions, Inc.